Gift of

REAL EMOTIONAL LOGIC

REAL
EMOTIONAL
LOGIC

Film and Television Docudrama
as Persuasive Practice

Steven N. Lipkin

Southern Illinois University Press
Carbondale and Edwardsville

Portions of chapter 2 were published in "*Quiz Show* as Persuasive Docudrama,"
from *www.imagesjournal.com/issue01/features/quiz.htm,* and in "Real Emotional
Logic: Persuasive Strategies in Docudrama," from *Cinema Journal* 38.4 (1999): 68–
85. Copyright © 1999 by the University of Texas Press. All rights reserved. Portions
of the interview material in chapter 5 originally were published in "The Politics of
Adaptation: Interview with Dennis Nemec and Tom Cook," from *Creative
Screenwriting* 4.4 (Winter 1997): 49–53. A portion of chapter 6 was published in
"When Victims Speak (or, What Happened When Spielberg Added *Amistad* to His
List?)" from *Journal of Film and Video* 52.4 (2001): 15–32.

Library of Congress Cataloging-in-Publication Data

Lipkin, Steven N., 1951–
  Real emotional logic : film and television docudrama as persuasive practice /
Steven N. Lipkin.
      p. cm.
  Includes bibliographical references and index.
  1. Historical films—United States—History and criticism. 2. Historical television
programs—United States—History and criticism. I. Title.

PN1995.9.H5 L56 2002
791.43'658—dc21
                                                                2001020549
  ISBN 0-8093-2409-1 (alk. paper)

Contents

Illustrations

Preface:
Based on a True Story

When the end credits for *Mississippi Burning* began to roll, my wife inadvertently planted one of the seeds for this book. She turned to me and asked if what we'd just seen was supposed to be a true story. We knew some of it was, some of it wasn't—what exactly were we supposed to distill from it? If we bought into the film's version of events, were we the ones who were going to end up getting burned?

When a work declares itself to be based on a "true story," we assume that it purports to represent events and people the way they "really" were. In light of the work's self-proclaimed association with the "truth," this is a logical presumption. It leads to the traditional view of docudrama that weighs the form on a scale calibrated with the values customarily applied to documents that have truth value, documents that we expect to contribute to the discourses of history. *Mississippi Burning* and the other docudramas I examined subsequently led me to realize that this approach to docudrama does not adequately account for the qualifier in the phrase "based on a true story." A docudrama's "basis" in truth actually launches the work in a different direction from straightforward documentation. Representation of the real is only part of what drives a docudrama; the work's other basic purpose is to envelop us in the experience of its story. The overall thrust of docudrama is neither exposition nor logical argumentation, but persuasion. Docudrama exists to create conviction. Docudrama strives to persuade us to believe that what occurred happened much as we see it on the screen.

In the wake of the releases in the early 1990s of *JFK* (Oliver Stone 1991) and *Schindler's List* (Steven Spielberg 1994), I started asking people if they thought that there was something especially compelling about films based on true stories. They said it was easier to believe in a story if its people and actions had a basis in actuality. It was intriguing to get the "inside story" about how things had "really" happened. It was easier to "relate to" what others had "really done," implying that something could be learned from the experiences shown because they had occurred in actuality. The comments indicate the importance of the combination of fiction and nonfiction, and narrative and actuality. They provided the starting points to determine how docudramas were persuasive and why.

Since I began this research, the first three germinal, introductory studies of docudrama proper have appeared. Alan Rosenthal's *Writing Docudrama* addresses considerations that the form raises for potential scriptwriters. His subsequent anthology, *Why Docudrama?*, marks the wide spectrum of basic issues relevant to the history and manifestation of docudramatic material in both film and TV. Derek Paget's *No Other Way to Tell It: Dramadoc/Docudrama on Television* provides invaluable insights into the formation of television docudrama, particularly in Great Britain, where, as Rosenthal also points out, there exists an earlier and more extensively developed tradition than in the United States for hybrid presentational modes.

As works of persuasive power, docudramas ride the fence between narrative and documentary, blending the strategies of both, belonging wholly to neither. Documentary studies without considering docudramas as such may mention moments in the history of nonfiction film noteworthy for their dependence on re-creation (turn-of-the-century newsreels, the films of Sergei Eisenstein, the British World War II home front films of Humphrey Jennings, "postmodernist" documentaries).[1] The exclusion of docudrama from documentary seems proper, since even a documentary dependent upon re-creation places subject over story, and does not necessarily balance both documentary and fictional narrative strategies. Fiction film studies similarly avoid docudrama as a genre. Docudramas are prone to be subordinated within other narrative categories, such as the "historical film," the biopic, or film noir.[2]

If docudrama's merging of elements of narration and documentary results in such an appealing form of storytelling, then what is the evidence of that appeal? The frequency of docudrama production and reception shows how attractive docudrama argument has become to its audience.[3] Rosenthal already has placed on the table the question of the usefulness of the form. He suggests it offers a glimpse of otherwise inaccessible, actual subjects made more appealing by the understanding that these events "really" happened. (*Writing* 20–23) It remains to investigate in depth how the appeal of docudrama inheres within its very form of presentation.

A few years and as many docudramas after screening *Mississippi Burning*, this project started out focusing on feature films "based on" true stories. I eventually included movie-of-the-week (MOW) docudrama because it became clear that the structure and purposes of the two longer forms had a great deal in common. Shorter form, "reality TV" programs might share a basis in "true stories" but tell them differently. Reality TV programs have developed an alternative means of delivery to the long form narrative characteristic of docudrama as I define it here. Long form docudramas present to us a distinct kind of persuasive practice. Consequently, each chapter of this book places the methods of persuasion under study in the context of specific cases that illustrate docudrama's persuasive strategies at work. This case study approach begins by situating docudrama as a mode of presentation, a synthesis of documentary and narrative forms that functions as persuasive argument, and subsequently examines its strategies in the contexts of feature film and MOW discourse.

Chapter 1, "Defining Docudrama," reviews existing definitions of the mode and identifies and describes the commonalities that could connect works as ostensibly different as *Schindler's List* and *In the Name of the Father* (Jim Sheridan 1994). To understand docudrama as persuasive practice requires, first, a description of docudrama form that not only defines but also describes how it functions as persuasive argument. Docudrama stories are told through the melodramatic staging of documentary material. Arguments put to persuasive purpose consist of data (evidence), claims (what the argument advocates), and warrants (the connections between claims and evidence). These are elements of a standard model of argument and will provide a framework for the analysis of texts throughout this study.[4] *Schindler's List* and *In the Name of the Father* in this chapter illustrate how docudrama places actuality within melodramatic terms as a means of persuasive argument.

Chapter 2, "All the Good Reasons," examines in more detail the strategies that allow for the docudramatic warranting of persuasive arguments. Works with a basis in prior, known events, actions, and people refer to data already in the public record. They assert moral positions that ultimately become claims made by the film's narrative and warrant these claims through formal strategies that bring together re-creation and actuality.[5] Docudrama form foregrounds the process of warranting—legitimating—persuasive argument. Docudrama's reason for being is to do precisely what warrants do, that is, to show that a logical relationship exists between data and the claims the argument advocates. This chapter explores the basic means by which docudrama establishes connections between actuality and filmic re-creation, between the known and the speculative. It finds a precedent for the style of persuasive argument in today's film and

MOW docudramas in Twentieth Century–Fox's cycle of postwar semi-documentaries.

Docudrama has a history but is more problematic in the way that it presents the past. Chapter 3, "Dramatic Evidence," asks if, regardless of the strength of its warrants, docudrama form detracts from the view of history it presents. Historiographers, who consider narrative as one of a number of a means of conveying a sense of the past, suggest that any writing of history necessarily reformulates the primary experience of the time it documents. In this view the key historiographic issue is not "factuality" as much as it is honesty of form of presentation.[6] This chapter examines how docudrama's foregrounding of moments depicted as the intersection of personal and historical time make historical process accessible. Chapter 4, "Docudrama Ethics and the Problem of Proximity," subsequently considers how proximity of source material has implications for the ethics involved when docudrama forwards its view of historical material.

Docudrama stories couch novel, unfamiliar dimensions of actualities in what become literally "familiar" terms, depending upon the basic structures, the figures and conflicts, of melodrama. Accordingly, docudrama's persuasive argument, in the spirit of melodrama, ultimately restores a sense of order to a seemingly chaotic universe, using narrative to provide moral clarification. The way the moral view of melodrama is ideologically rooted is examined in the two concluding sections of this book. Chapter 5, "Rootable, Relatable, Promotable Docudrama," turns to TV writers, producers, and network executives to detail how they have conceived and produced MOW docudrama. The notion of "relatability" emerges from their thinking as central to the industry's selection, shaping, and marketing of MOW material. Case studies show how MOW docudrama has adapted the character/conflict/closure narrative structure of the classic Hollywood cinema into victim/trial/articulation configurations as it tells stories based on "relatability."

Through the 1990s, the industry has continued regularly to make feature films based on true stories. The last chapter, "Recent Feature Film Docudrama as Persuasive Practice," begins by comparing late 1990s feature films with MOW docudramas. It compares MOW rhetorical strategies with those operating in the substantial groups of feature film docudramas distributed in 1997, including *Donnie Brasco* (Mike Newell); *Shine* (Scott Hicks); *The People Vs. Larry Flynt* (Milos Forman); *Ghosts of Mississippi* (Rob Reiner); *Rosewood* (John Singleton); *Amistad* (Steven Spielberg); and in 1999, *A Civil Action* (Steven Zaillan); *At First Sight* (Irwin Winkler); *Hilary and Jackie* (Anand Tucker); *Patch Adams* (Tom

Shadyac); *Music of the Heart* (Wes Craven); and *October Sky* (Joe Johnston). The main points of comparison include what relatability strategies are in these works and how these strategies instruct their filmic and extra-filmic audiences, particularly as they position spectators in relation to the docu-dramatic presentation of character, community, and text. These features favor stories about men and, consequently, vary from their MOW cousins by centering on male rather than female victim/survivors and their trials. Communities appear consistently in these films as audiences. Their witnessing, their acts of spectatorship, instruct our own.

Contemporary docudrama features and comparable MOWs illustrate how this mode of presentation offers attractive instruction for a substantial audience. The recurrence of film and television docudrama indicates the extent to which the mode has become an important means of presenting persuasive argument in our culture. The very prominence, if not notoriety, of docudrama titles in the 1990s shows that these are works that tell stories that we need, works that, as their label indicates, make compelling arguments because they bring documents to dramatic life.

This book never would have come into existence without the ongoing support of my colleagues in the Department of Communication. Many others have been equally important to the realization of this project. First and foremost, I must thank Alan Rosenthal for his years of the most generous, invaluable advice and guidance a friend could provide. I am also deeply indebted to Derek Paget and Charles Affron for their rich insights and great companionship. Debbie Amelon, Nancy Bein, and Cynthia Cherbak facilitated my research on the West Coast. For sharing their time and the wisdom of their experiences in creating much of the work this book is about, I must thank Tom Cook, Dennis Nemec, Charles Freericks, Abby Tetenbaum, Steve Sohmer, Dave Caldwell, Victoria Sterling, Victoria Bazely, Phil Krupp, Tristine Rainer, Bruce Miller, and Michael Laskin. Abby, Liz, and Isaac Tetenbaum have been gracious and patient hosts. I am grateful to Jim Simmons and the editorial staff at Southern Illinois University Press for the time and care they have given this work. Finally, I thank my family for helping me keep the right goals clearly in sight.

REAL EMOTIONAL LOGIC

1 | Defining Docudrama: *Schindler's List* and *In the Name of the Father*

The presumptions underlying the production of a docudrama suggest that its story "should" be told, and that re-creation of actual events remains the best if not the only means of delivery. Films "based on true stories" such as *Schindler's List* (Steven Spielberg 1994) and *In the Name of the Father* (Jim Sheridan 1994) exemplify the indexical roots, the melodramatic coding, and the consequent moral and ethical problematic that require attention as primary defining elements of docudrama.

As its name suggests, "docudrama" is a hybrid form, wedding "documentary" material with "drama," particularly melodrama. Definitions of docudrama others have offered emphasize the problem of the form's merger of fiction and nonfiction modes.[1] Jane Feuer, in her discussion of movie-of-the-week "trauma dramas," writes that they "take the form of the docudrama, by definition a narrative representation of 'real people' and 'real events'" (20). Daniel Leab cites Michael Arlen's definition, that a docudrama is "a hybrid form . . . a story whose energy and focus have shifted from fiction to what is supposed to have actually happened" (78). Tom Hoffer and Richard A. Nelson begin their overview of TV docudrama by defining it as a "presentation of real-life contemporary problems in dramatic fashion on television" (64). After a thorough review of the root terms that constitute the labels "docudrama," "dramatic documentary," and "dramadoc," Derek Paget concludes that "in drama-documentary the drama diverts the documentary element into dramatic structuring; in documentary drama the documentary diverts the drama into documentary structures" (114). I will take up below the concern for the interrelationship of presentational structure and documentary material Paget's comments reflect. For now, "docudrama," the term I will use here, places "drama" at the root of the form, suggesting the "docu" prefix assumes a position of qualifying, rather than preempting or replacing that root function.[2] The description of docudramatic form I will develop centers on how, distinct from conventional documentaries, docudramas replace indexical, "unstaged" images with a quasi-indexical narrative. Image and story claim a motivated, direct relationship to the events the film references. The docudrama narrative, moreover, foregrounds dramatic codes, assuming melodrama's larger function of emphatically clarifying a broad moral system through domestic imagery.

The Indexical Roots of Docudrama

The status of docudrama relative to documentary proper remains problematic for a number of reasons. It is inviting to view a docudrama as a pseudodocument that would strive to lay claim to historical truth but follows the more marketable path of mass fiction. Changes in the technology of film/video documentation since World War II raise epistemological as well as ethical questions about the choice of a re-creative mode, if one's purpose remains the evaluation of the work as document. Not surprisingly, past work in the two areas of scholarship that have given docudrama some specific consideration, historical feature film studies and documentary theory, have tended to view "docudrama" primarily in relation to the functions of "documents." As a consequence of its place between fiction and documentary modes, the form of "docudrama," the ways and means by which it blends modes, has not been as important in this literature as what happens to "history" in the historical film, or what the relationship of film documents are to the subjects they represent. Studies of the historical film have focused on the historiographic issues raised by the representation of the past in feature films. Documentary studies examine the fidelity of representation. A brief survey can illustrate the concerns of the two traditions. In presenting the "historiographic" approach, Daniel Leab, for example, devotes several pages to the distortions of history that inevitably arise from docudrama form (78–87). His overview exemplifies what Jane Feuer terms the "elitist" critique of docudrama (21). George Custen's study of the biopic approaches this kind of film as a means of representing history. Custen examines in depth the processing of public history by classic Hollywood narrative film style as it produced biographical fact-based fiction. Extensive treatments of the more general problems inherent in the representation of history in fiction films have appeared in a number of works and will receive further attention in chapter 3. Hayden White focuses on the necessity of representing history by means of narration, suggesting the narrative act itself ultimately asserts what is meaningful regarding the history in question. Robert Rosenstone (in *Revisioning History* and *Visions of the Past*) clarifies how invention is necessary in both filmed as well as written history and illustrates how strategies of alteration, condensation, and anachronism characterize historical portrayals in any medium. An exchange between Robert Burgoyne and Angela Dalle-Vacche broaches issues of history portrayed phenomenologically, noting the impact of the cinematic rendering of order, frequency, and duration on the resulting view of history in Bertolucci's *1900*.[3]

Docudrama has been equally problematic for documentary historians and theorists. If the "historiographic" view monitors what happens to "history" in these features, the documentary theorists similarly address the implications of the form when it represents the real. Jack Ellis's history of documentary discusses several points at which fiction and nonfiction film forms overlap or intersect each other, including the turn toward story form in Direct Cinema; however, he does not consider dramatic re-creation as a sub-form of documentary in its own right. John Corner does relate docudrama briefly to "dramadocs" (31, 34) but primarily is concerned with the latter, defining them, as does Paget, as documentaries that utilize re-creation and narrative strategies. Several of the essays in Michael Renov's *Theorizing Documentary* examine the impact of narrative structures on the functions of the documentary mode. Renov's own introductory essay to the anthology examines the dependence of documentary on narrative (6). Philip Rosen's "Document and Documentary" argues that any filmic representation is, at best, a constructed simulation of the real, suggesting that unstaged images have issues of authenticity just as do recreations (82). Paul Arthur observes that "American documentaries have never marshalled a serious challenge to the hegemony of fiction film in the representation of social reality" (108). Carl Plantinga, in taking up similar issues growing out of the constructed nature of documentary signs (*Rhetoric* 64), acknowledges the "fuzzy boundaries" (12) that often exist between fiction and nonfiction modes as they represent the real. Plantinga's concern is not so much to clarify the "fuzzy" as it is to explore how the nature of nonfiction films stems from the way they position their viewer to understand that a "nonfiction film asserts or implies that the states of affairs it presents occur in the actual world as portrayed" (86). As a documentary theorist, Bill Nichols perhaps makes clearest why docudrama cannot be documentary. In *Representing Reality,* Nichols maintains an absolute, systematic distinction between documentary (building its cases from materials of the historical world) and fiction (constructed from materials that can only resemble the historical world metaphorically). Nichols's efforts to define documentary preclude any consideration of the "truth value" of docudrama, since its re-creations relegate the form without mitigation to the realm of fiction.

The "historical film" and "documentary theorist" views of docudrama issues understandably share making primary their concerns for how films represent the real, whether it be past or present. Both views explain films, whether they are historical features or nonfiction representations, in relation to their potential documentary functions. This allows only a partial assessment of how docudrama works, however, because it privileges one part of docudrama's form, the actuality that provides the premise of the docudrama story, rather than seeing how narrative and nonfiction elements interrelate in an overall system. What both the historical film and documentary theorist views neglect is that docudrama is using narrative structure to advocate its view of its subject; in docudrama the narrative components of character, conflict, and resolution cannot be separated from the view of actuality they forward.

Even if on these terms docudrama does not assert documentary truth values about the historical world, it still maintains a close connection to documentary. Docudrama argues with the seriousness of documentary to the extent that it draws upon direct, motivated resemblances to its actual materials. As fictions, docudramas offer powerful, attractive persuasive arguments about actual subjects, depicting people, places, actions, and events that exist or have existed. To borrow a page from Nichols, it is on the basis of its close resemblances to actuality that docudrama argues for the validity of its metaphors. The stories of docudrama attempt to persuade us with a logic of motivated iconicity.

Even as docudrama departs from documentary proper, the two modes retain a certain semiotic similarity. The evolving technology of mainstream documentary progressively has aligned representation and actuality. The documentary image functions as an index. Comparable imagery in docudrama remains primarily iconic; however, docudrama asks if, under its terms, the two signs might not be all that different.[4] The films' often high degree of resemblance to actual people, places, actions, and events suggests that docudramatic imagery combines characteristics of iconic and indexical signs, creating what amount to indexical icons, signs with direct, strongly motivated resemblances to their actual referents. We are offered argument-by-analogy, the analogies (images) often appearing of the most literal kind.

The docudrama narrative may also reference other, earlier texts that offer the initial definition of their actual material. The very existence of a prior text or texts arguably motivates production of the film, as well as its eventual narrative structure. The viewer is invited to accept the argument that re-creation warrants, that what we see might have "really" happened in "much this way." The notion of warranting is particularly helpful here, since a warrant locates the basis in common knowledge, common sense, and/or rules of logic that allow an argument to make the necessary shift from fact to value.[5]

In the case of film docudrama, warranting occurs both in the choice of subject and in the choice of mode of presentation. The strength of the argument-by-analogy the film's indexical icons will make must depend upon these warrants. The warrants forward the claims the film will make, essentially, the moral position of the film's melodramatic coding.

Docudramas stem from "known" events and figures. The previous text or texts tend to include news stories, published accounts, and personal testimonies such as Thomas Keneally's novel about Oskar Schindler, Gerry Conlon's printed exposé of his case, or Jim Garrison's view of the Kennedy assassination.[6] The existence of prior text/narrative warrants the choice of material for filmic treatment: These events "really" happened and were important enough for reportage. We are asked to consider that they might have happened "this" way, in the version now offered as feature film docudrama. The choice of the docudramatic mode of presentation itself offers a second warrant. "Actual" documentary materials either do not exist or by themselves are incomplete or insufficient to treat the subject adequately.

Its premises secured, melodramatic form delivers the docudrama's ultimate moral judgments on its material. Film melodrama places domestic settings and familial imagery within the context of larger social systems revealed in the narrative as powerful and corrupt, repressive to the point of hellishness.[7] The often excessive depiction of domestic life caught up in a constraining, destructive world of social power allows the melodramatic narrative to pronounce emphatically through its re-created actual material a clear moral perspective. Like melodrama generally, docudrama suggests that lost moral structures can be recovered and restored. While the actuality the work re-creates may show the exercise of right and wrong thrown into jeopardy, the treatment of actual people, incidents, and events in the docudrama ultimately allows a literal moral "refamiliarization," a restoration of a moral system in the universe.[8]

Docudrama as Melodrama

As different as they are in scope and subject matter, *Schindler's List* and *In the Name of the Father* are comparable in arguing that injustice results when social systems go wrong. In the mode of melodrama, *Schindler's List* and *In the Name of the Father* examine how destructive social powers applied against weak, domestically imaged victims produce explicitly hellish results. The exercise of power accordingly appears random and arbitrary, the viciousness of persecution commensurate with the lack of underlying reason.

In the Name of the Father renders the British legal process in images of powerless individuals trapped by large, impersonal, impervious, monolithic instruments of social control. Gerry Conlon, Giuseppi Conlon, and Paul Hill are arrested, interrogated, tried, convicted, and incarcerated because they are Irishmen by chance in the wrong places at the wrong times. Social environments funnel claustrophobically from city streets in Ireland to those in London, to an English courtroom, to the jail in which both Conlons are incarcerated. Images of the Conlons' surroundings feature overpowering vertical lines often viewed subjectively (the buildings of the Conlons' home turf surrounded by the massed British army; the spectators, advocates, and judges in the courtroom scenes; the barred walls of the multitiered prison) (see figs. 1 and 2). After a riot, the jail that wrongfully imprisons the Conlons becomes even more tightly barred. The film's series of constraining environments progressively shows how the legal system eliminates individual movement and self-determination. The film depicts injustice as the erroneous suppression of individuality by an increasingly purgatorial system.

To the image of life under the Nazis as wrongful incarceration, *Schindler's List* adds the phenomenon of "selection" and develops throughout the film its moral consequences. "Selection" of Jews for deportation, liquidation (of the Cracow ghetto), and final annihilation in the gas chambers of Auschwitz remains a given from the film's opening sequences so that the issue is never why Jews have been selected for destruction but which ones will be chosen and with what consequences. The horror of pending death and destruction begins with the irrationally random selection process.

The film's opening explicitly links Judaic culture with the iconography of selection, chaos, death, and destruction. The *Shabbat* candle lit in the opening scene burns out as the prayer for candle lighting finishes. The end of candle and prayer raise a question appropriate to the beginning of a film about Jews in Germany during World War II: What will happen to God in the absence of the rituals, the culture, and the believers that sustain His existence? We are at the advent of a truly "desacralized" world, a world from which most forms of the sacred have been banished (Brooks 5). The smoke of the *Shabbat* candle tapers upward as the image dissolves into the smoke of a railroad engine at a station where the soon frequently seen folding tables are set up for processing deportees.

To underline the consequences of selection, smoke appears throughout the film at key junctures, seen, for example, hovering over the "liquidated" Cracow ghetto from burning debris and gunshots. Arbitrary Nazi persecution appears drawn from an inferno. Ash drops on shoulders and car fenders later as the same victims are exhumed and cremated. Nazi soldiers scream and cackle insanely while they build into blazing pyres stacks of decomposing bodies bulldozed up from the mass graves holding the dead of the ghetto. Near the film's end, Auschwitz is shown *Night and Fog*–like from the front gate, smoke belching from its infamous ovens.

In each environment, the matter of "selection," the choice of who will live and who will die, is emphatically arbitrary, underlining the horrific chaos at the core of the ostensibly orderly Nazi-run society. Jews are doubly damned, since they must collaborate in the selection process in order to survive at all. Many receive the precious, lifesaving "blue cards" that verify "essential worker status" only because they are known to Stern, the *Judenrat* leader Oskar Schindler enlists to help administer his enterprise.

Stern's "selections" promote survival. Nazi selection procedures by contrast place arbitrary, irrational violence under the facade of orderly lines and bureaucratic trappings. Amon Goeth, the Nazi commandant running the Plaszgow camp that has become the new "home" of the displaced ghetto residents, stands on his balcony with a telescopically sighted rifle and picks off camp interees at random. The ultimate horror intimated throughout the film, then finally shown, remains "selection" for the gas chambers at Auschwitz.

Within their enormously repressive, arbitrarily destructive, hellish social settings, *In the Name of the Father* and *Schindler's List* erect fundamentally melodramatic narrative structures. The lens of melodrama brings a moral clarity to the brutish violence the films show destructive social powers inflicting upon helpless victims. Both films place characters within familial and/or domestic settings, employing father figures to mediate moral perspectives. Gerry Conlon moves through a succession of literal or figurative families in the course of the film. He and Paul Hill are assisted in their escape from the British army at the film's opening by the people of their neighborhood. Their route takes them through homes and yards. Conlon leaves his home in Ireland and takes up temporarily with a hippie commune in London; subsequently, his trials become prosecutions of both his actual and surrogate families, as his blood relatives captured at his aunt's flat as well as the members of the commune are tried as terrorists. When Conlon and his father are jailed, the other inmates form a final surrogate family, complete with another surrogate father (the actual IRA bomber who has confessed to the murders Conlon and Hill have been convicted of). Conlon "returns" to embrace fully the importance of his father's self-sacrifice. Conlon is ultimately redeemed through the late-found desire to save his "real" father, to right the wrong the system has perpetrated against him.

Schindler's List also features contrasting family settings and even more extremely contrasting father figures. Oskar Schindler and Amon Goeth are morally opposite surrogates of the same "family," the Jews of Cracow. Settings in this film also move through a succession of domestic environments: People are displaced from their original residences and forced to cram together by the dozens, first in reassigned ghetto apartments, then the Plaszgow camp barracks. Schindler's factory provides an opportunity to survive the dangers of the ghetto or the camp. Its imagery turns domestic. The factory manufactures pots and pans. Schindler eats at a table in a corner of his upstairs office, surrounded by houseplants (see fig. 3). As a melodramatic icon, the factory stairway figures prominently in the film when a woman comes to Schindler twice to beg him to take on her father and mother as workers. He stands at the top of the stairs, a backlit, smoke-enshrouded figure of mystery, his life-granting power verified in a subsequent scene when the daughter stands across the street, watching unseen, Stella Dallas–like as her parents arrive for work.

By contrast, the house of Goeth, quite literally a house on the edge of the Plaszgow camp, consistently and perversely marks its domestic spaces with the ongoing processes of repression, terror, and death (see fig. 4). In yet another selection scene (eerily evocative of Schindler interviewing secretarial candidates), Goeth chooses his maid out of a lineup of possibilities drawn from his available interees. Helen works "downstairs," a domestic/kitchen area in which she receives successive "visits" from both Schindler and Goeth. Schindler endows her with "not that kind of kiss" and some paternal encouragement. Goeth, he assures her, needs her too much ever to kill her. Subsequently, when Goeth "visits" Helen in her domestic realm, he does not murder her but assaults her, then backs away, leaving the threat of the exercise of his absolute power intact.

The "upstairs" of Goeth's house stages a succession of decadent dinner parties for Goeth's army and civilian acquaintances and, most predominantly, allows us into his bedroom with its balcony overlooking his realm. From here he shoots interees and discusses the rigors of his job with his bedmate. The fusion of bedroom, bed, half-naked mistress, sunlit balcony, and random snipings characterize his patriarchy by his intertwined venting of sexual and murderous physical aggression.

Goeth's status as a patriarchal bully is underlined by his victims, who tend to be women, children, or men made submissively childlike. A female engineer who is not intimidated by him is shot, apparently because of her competence. An equally competent hinge-maker's very competence is viewed twistedly as prima facie evidence that he's slacked off, reducing the man to pray for his life to be spared (and it is, when, once again, chance intervenes and none of Goeth's available pistols will work). Goeth appears to follow Schindler's advice to exercise forgiveness as the most absolute form of power when he confronts Lisiek, a boy who works as another of his servants, with stains still not removed from the bathtub. He tells Lisiek "I forgive you" but shoots him anyway as the boy is crossing the parade ground reentering the camp.

Schindler's workers are similarly childlike in their deference to him (he orders Stern to keep away from him workers such as the one-armed old man who wants to thank Schindler for his job) or are literally children (such as a quick-witted boy who saves a large group from execution for stealing a chicken, or a girl who brings Schindler a birthday cake and whom he kisses, resulting in his incarceration by the SS).

Schindler's status as "good" father is warranted by his shift from selfishness to self-sacrifice. He is characterized initially in the film by his material superficiality. Before we see him, we meet him through his clothing (his suits, shirts, and ties, which are being laid out), his cuff links and watch, his money clip, and, last, his Nazi party pin. He tells Stern he needs someone with a head for business to run his company, to free him to concentrate on "presentation."

Stern acts as the alchemist's stone, the means of eventual transformation that turns Schindler from petty capitalist to self-sacrificing humanist. Stern's selfless work to save others provides Schindler with an infectious moral reference. Stern knows business and knows the Jewish populace upon which Schindler must depend for the slave labor that will allow his immense profits. Schindler himself must intervene, however, when Stern is swept up and loaded on a train for deportation. He effects a last-minute rescue, and from that point of direct involvement, Schindler progressively sheds the material his workers have allowed him to gain in order to keep his workforce intact. Schindler trades his saddle (from which he watched the liquidation of the ghetto), lighter, watch, jewels, and entire suitcases of currency for human beings. By the time he has liquidated his own possessions in order to save all of his workers, he knows eleven hundred of their names. Early on in his enterprise, he considers a shot worker as "lost time" and governmental "compensation"; by the war's end, he is faced with the fact of the entire group, standing before him, and he grieves: "This car! Why did I keep it? I could have saved two people! Two people!"

The conclusion of *Schindler's List* offers a final warranting of its docu-dramatic articulation by wedding the moral perspective conveyed through its narrative's melodrama with a succession of documentary images and assertions. The group of Schindler's Jews we see at the conclusion of the story walks over a hill, and their image dissolves to color, present-day foot-age of the actual survivors of this same group. In a fusion of document and melodrama, as each film actor escorts the real-life person (or their spouse or child) that they played in the film to Oskar Schindler's grave, subtitles inform us that Schindler died a business failure more than twenty years after the war's end, that he is buried in Israel, and that while today a total of four thousand Jews survive in Poland, there are over six thou-sand descendants of Schindler's Jews. Thus, the pictorial and statistical evidence of the group's existence today warrants the view the film we've just seen offers of its subject.[9]

The docudramas considered here draw power from similar strategies. They reference actual people and events through melodramatic narrative codes. The evil of monolithic social power stems from its random, arbi-trarily murderous exercise. The evil abuse of power in Nazi society is ren-dered in *Schindler's List* by random choices of victims to be murdered. The same kind of monolithic social power is portrayed in *In the Name of the Father* as a corrupt, arbitrary, abusive judicial process. "Good" characters within these worlds begin as flawed heroes "saved" when they can become redeemed by freedom from self-absorption. Schindler becomes a "good" father when he sheds his materiality; Gerry Conlon learns to transfer his concerns and energies from himself to his own father, who has already sacrificed his health and freedom out of his concern for his son.

As docudramas, *Schindler's List* and *In the Name of the Father* argue melodramatically for the worth of thought about their subjects. The films offer alternatives to the kind of sober discourse about history that would be the province of documentary. They operate as artistic perceptions of history, offering viewers the opportunity to share the film artists' reflec-tions upon the historical material the works represent. On these terms, the films allow a sense of closeness to that history, an access made pos-sible by rendering chaotic, destructive horrors understandable as essen-tially domestic conflicts escalated to vastly larger social scales. The films suggest worlds from which morality has been lost, then restored. Proximity to the factual in the films attempts to root artistic vision within the sober ground of historical actuality, suggesting at the same time that good has come out of suffering, that justice has prevailed, that as it must in melodrama, some order has been restored to a chaotic universe.

2 | All the Good Reasons: Persuasive Warrants and Moral Claims

The semi-documentary surfaces of *House on 92d Street, 13 Rue Madeleine,* and *Call Northside 777* can be dismissed as a passing fancy of the American cinema.
—Andrew Sarris, *The American Cinema*

D ue to the hybrid nature of its form, docudrama demands a particular kind of suspension of disbelief from its audience. The docudrama viewer becomes immersed in a blend of documentary and melodrama. One's involvement begins by accepting certain hypothetical premises implicit in this coupling. We are asked to accept that in this case, re-creation is a necessary mode of presentation. If we accept the historical substance of pre-filmic events, then we are also asked to grant that these might have happened in much the way we are about to see them depicted.

The last chapter proposed that re-creation and fictionalization will warrant—justify—the film's argument to the extent that the resulting docudrama indicates its connections to actuality. This chapter will identify some of those links between actuality and re-creation and show how they function as warrants in docudrama argument. Despite Andrew Sarris's dismissal of the cycle of docudramas produced at Twentieth Century–Fox (TCF) immediately after World War II, these films offer earlier models of a contemporary docudramatic logic, based on anchors to actuality that establish a style of argument characteristic of today's film and television docudramas. Robert Redford's *Quiz Show* (1994) and Penny Marshall's *A League of Their Own* (1992) will provide evidence of how the warranting strategies evident in TCF's postwar "semi-documentaries" are at work in more recent feature films.

This effort to describe docudrama rhetoric and to situate it historically assumes that docudrama functions importantly as argument. A model of argument will offer one means to describe the basic elements of docudrama form. Consistent with its functions as melodrama, a film in this mode not only advocates a moral truth in its re-presentation of the actual people, places, events, and actions at its source but also serves up an argument highly appealing to its audience. The form's popularity offers some of the strongest evidence of its effectiveness and its pervasive influence as a means of ideological reinforcement.

The films examined here will show three basic ways that warrants can link data (the evidence upon which an argument is built) with claims (the position the argument advocates).[1] These links indicate the proximity of data and claims through strategies I will term modeling, sequencing, and interaction. Models reconstruct their referents iconically.[2] Sequences arrange actual and re-created shots and scenes in succession. Interactions place actual and re-created filmic elements together within a scene. Models, sequences, and interactions are products of cinematic articulation. They establish warranting strategies because the varying types of proximities they provide allow pictorial and spatial inferences. As strategies, these three basic means of relating data and claims encourage a connection between document and drama, and the known and the speculative. The tighter the link, the more solid the premise and the more potentially appealing the film's argument. TCF's postwar docudramas offer a fruitful case study because of the priority the studio placed on actuality in much of its product, and the resulting films' foregrounding of their previous texts.

TCF's Commitment to Actuality

Rather than simply providing the "passing fancy" that Andrew Sarris claims, Hollywood's production of docudrama preceded TCF's 1940s actuality films and continued subsequently.[3] Within broad, ongoing groups of narratives tending to draw on actual material (war films, history films, gangster films, social "problem" films, biopics), notable examples of "realistic" contemporary social issues narratives can be found offered in each decade before World War II (*A Corner in Wheat* [D. W. Griffith 1909]; *Traffic in Souls* [George L. Tucker 1913]; *The Crowd* [King Vidor 1928]; *I Was a Fugitive from a Chain Gang* [Mervyn Le Roy 1932]; *Fury* [Fritz Lang 1936]; *Grapes of Wrath* [John Ford 1940]) and afterward (*On the Waterfront* [Elia Kazan 1954]; *Blackboard Jungle* [Richard Brooks 1955]; *The Man with the Golden Arm* [Otto Preminger 1955]).[4] The production and consumption of documentaries during World War II prepared filmmakers and audiences for stories confronting contemporary historical circumstances. The availability of works of Italian neorealism (*Rome,*

Open City 1945, *Paisan* 1946) also suggests that the immediate postwar film culture was receptive to the docudramatic mode.[5]

Within the industry's maintenance of docudrama as a mode of narrative, a more specific source of the TCF cycle is Darryl F. Zanuck's predilection for actuality-based story material.[6] At least some of the seeds of TCF's cycle of postwar docudrama production had been planted at several points earlier in Zanuck's career when he oversaw the production of films tackling "serious" and current subject matter. Through the early 1930s, as a staff writer turned Warner Brothers head of production, Zanuck would see the commercial success of diverse stories drawing on contemporary social tensions, such as crime *(Little Caesar; Public Enemy)*, poverty *(42nd Street)*, and ethnicity *(The Jazz Singer)*. When Zanuck subsequently assumed control of TCF, the "headline" subjects characteristic of these Warner Brothers works gave way to literary adaptations also steeped in social issues sure to resonate with contemporary audiences, such as *Les Miserables* (1935), *The Grapes of Wrath* (1940), and *How Green Was My Valley* (1941) (Custen, *Fox* 14).[7] Zanuck's work making documentaries during his World War II enlistment (Custen, *Fox* 2) strengthened his desire to make films subsequently dealing with serious subjects that would still reach large audiences (265).[8] In this context, TCF's docudramas took a logical turn to location shooting after the war:[9]

> In making *The House on 92nd Street* and *Call Northside 777*, [Zanuck] was among the first studio heads after World War II to take his crews on location. Because of his own experience with documentary production in the army, he knew how to use locations to capture gritty reality. Zanuck's mixture of realism and documentary techniques made these the forerunner of today's docudramas. (2)

Film histories have classified TCF's postwar docudramas as both social problem films and films noirs. *Call Northside 777* (1948) was the third docudrama Henry Hathaway directed for TCF after World War II. Hathaway made the first two (*The House on 92nd Street* 1945; *13 Rue Madeleine* 1946) with producer Louis de Rochemont, brought on board at Fox to apply his *March of Time* style to Hollywood feature production.[10] This cycle of docudramas was part of the larger group of postwar social problem films released predominantly by Fox that also included a trio of Elia Kazan films (*Gentleman's Agreement* 1947; *Boomerang!* 1947; and *Pinky* 1949). Fox's actuality films consisted of composite adaptations as well as features based on single cases. Both of these categories included stories of fictional origins, such as Laura Hobson's *Gentleman's Agreement*, and those with sources in actual material. For example, a number of FBI cases combined to form the basis for *The House on 92nd Street*.

Both *Boomerang!* and *Call Northside 777* were based on single, specific actual stories. The release of *Boomerang!* and *Northside* in consecutive years suggests that TCF saw the potential miscarriage of justice by a corrupt, inefficient system as one of a number of "hot" social issues that invited feature film exploitation within the larger market for realistic social drama. Trailers for *Northside* suggest furthermore that TCF's marketing strategy foregrounded the notoriety of the previous texts that created public awareness of the "true stories" the films were based on. Prior, wide-reaching public knowledge of the film's subjects stemmed specifically from articles in *Reader's Digest* and *Time* magazine in years preceding the release of each film (see below).

Most Profitable Films Noirs Produced by TCF, 1945–1949

Year	Title	Net Profit (millions)	TCF Ranking
1945	*House on 92nd Street*	$1.54	2
1946	*13 Rue Madeleine*	0.75	4
1947	*Boomerang!*	1.11	2
1948	*Gentleman's Agreement*	1.92	2
1948	*Call Northside 777*	1.26	3
1949	*Pinky*	2.60	1
1949	*Snake Pit*	1.46	3

Source: Data compiled from Solomon 221–22, 243–44.

TCF's postwar social problem films and films noirs reflect strategic efforts to exploit actuality. The studio's frequency and variety of production of these films indicates a response to a market affected by the war and ready to consume a more "reality"-anchored Hollywood vision.

From 1945 to 1949, TCF was a regular contributor to the number of films noirs produced and distributed by Hollywood studios,[11] films that used contemporary reality and urban settings in particular as key components of their visual style. Actuality-based films during the postwar years remained consistently one of the studio's most profitable products: *House on 92nd Street,* for example, was the studio's second best money maker in 1945 (a ranking shared by *Gentleman's Agreement,* the studio's highest grossing film of 1947); *Pinky* was the studio's highest grossing and most profitable film of 1949 (see table). Little wonder, then, that Zanuck wanted producer de Rochemont to augment the studio's exploitation of actuality-based material.

Critical Reception

In line with their strong performance at the box office, TCF's docudramas enjoyed a very favorable reception from film critics in a variety of popular and trade publications. Reviews hinge the importance of the films on their debt to documentary style, their topicality in bringing behind-the-scenes stories of the war to light or airing controversial social issues, and their probable influence on the stylistic future of Hollywood filmmaking.

Critics identified a number of sources of visual realism, including story sources. Reviews of the de Rochemont productions are uniformly quick to point out the films' understandable debt to newsreel reportorial style. The *New York Times* compares the look of *House on 92nd Street* to "battle documents" viewers would be familiar with (27 Sept. 1945: 24). For *Commonweal,* the film has "the same factual tone that pervades [de Rochemont's] March of Time shorts" (26 Sept. 1945: 576). *Variety* sees "the same off-screen documentary exposition" in *13 Rue Madeleine* helping to turn "yesterday's headlines" into "surefire" entertainment while showing audiences "how many facets went into the struggle for victory" (18 Dec. 1945: 14). *Film Daily* predicted the film's documentary technique would "click solidly" (19 Dec 1945: 8).

Reviews attributed consistently the atmosphere of actuality to documentary-inspired production methods, particularly shooting on locations where story events occurred, casting unknown or nonactors and actresses in many parts, and incorporating documentary footage into the narrative. The *New York Times,* for example, sees these techniques, including the casting of actual FBI agents, contributing to *House on 92nd Street's* "simple, terse manner which rings true and is, therefore, highly dramatic" (27 Sept. 1945: 24). Reviews of *Boomerang!,* based on a well-known, nationally publicized trial in Connecticut, also attend to the benefits gained by keeping the film production close to its actual sources. The *New Republic* notes that the location shooting and casting of *Boomerang!* give it that sharp excitement you can get from a newsreel—from watching the actions and reactions of people whose reality you don't question. All of the extras here and most of the bit parts are played with gusto by townspeople right off the streets of the typical small city where the action is laid. (17 Feb. 1947: 39)

The origins of both *Call Northside 777* and *Boomerang!* in news stories explains the reason for and the effectiveness of the extensive location shooting in both films. *Motion Picture Herald's* "Product Digest" detailed the specific Chicago locations used in *Call Northside,* including the Chicago Criminal Courts building, the South Wabash and South State "slums," and the state penitentiary in Joliet, Illinois (24 Jan. 1945: 4029). In order to demonstrate the verisimilitude of docudramatic modeling, *Life* provided its readers with brief photo studies that compare actual figures from the *House* and *Northside* stories to their re-created images in the films (1 Mar. 1948: 57–59; 8 Oct. 1945: 91–98).

The same elements were also vulnerable to critical backlash. "Realism" could create an Achilles heel if a reviewer felt melodrama overbalanced a film's impression of factuality. *Variety's* review of *Northside* faults Henry Hathaway's "retreat from the documentary form" in addition to a "jarring and unpersuasive performance" by James Stewart (21 June 1948: 8). (See also comments below on Cagney's performance in *13 Rue.*) The *New Yorker* consistently saw flawed verisimilitude in the entire group of Fox docudramas because of their attempted blending of documentary and melodrama, particularly in the "preposterous" depiction of foreign spies in New York City *(House on 92nd Street)* and the faulty presentation of journalistic technique in *Northside* (29 Sept. 1945: 70; 28 Feb. 1948: 56).

The representation of contemporary history more often, however, was viewed as a boost to a film's marketability. The reviews connect the visual "realism" of the TCF docudramas to their sources in recent headlines, emphasizing how story authenticity increases the attractiveness of close filmic re-creation. In its review of *House on 92nd Street, Variety* reports that "recently, it was revealed by 20th-Fox that it had a film which would be the first full-length feature to tell of the atomic bomb. 'House' is purportedly that film" (12 Sept. 1945: 16). Only "partially fictional" (*Newsweek* 24 Sept. 1945: 94), the film's narrative line was drawn from "a selection of the [FBI's] better experiences" (*Time* 8 Oct. 1945: 96). (*Time* goes on to point out that *House* contains "only 35 feet of film" shot in the studio.) *Commonweal* lauded the sequences shot with concealed cameras in New York City (28 Sept. 1945: 577). The film's timeliness, in *Film Daily's* view, offered "limitless exploitation possibilities" (13 Sept. 1945: 6), while

Motion Picture Herald concurred that with only a few weeks elapsed since the atomic bombing of Japan, the potential to create interest in the story's "hitherto undisclosed angles of the [bomb's] development" would be "exceptional" ("Product Digest" 15 Sept. 1945: 2645). In the first line of its review of *13 Rue Madeleine, Time* notes that this film, like *House,* is "culled from the war-time hush-hush files of the Office of Strategic Services" and accordingly, producer de Rochemont once again has been able "to put realistic punch into his entertainment" (6 Jan. 1947: 89). On a similar note, *Variety* observed that *Rue* succeeds by "utilizing New England and Quebec sites in the main, but there is nothing about the film that doesn't indicate super-Hollywood standards" (18 Dec. 1946: 14). The first half of the story, which covers the training of the agents with "newsreel exactitude" (*New York Times* 16 Jan. 1947: 30), impressed most critics more than the turn toward "melodrama" in the second half, when James Cagney's performance in the film's lead weakened as the story pushed toward its climax.[12]

In noting how "realism" is a logical product of the use of current events and social issues for story material, reviewers felt that the turn toward narrating contemporary reality served audience needs and interests. Films such as *House* and *13 Rue Madeleine* offer a necessary kind of "now it can be told" explanation of how America was able to win the war.[13] Taking on social problem topics indicates the courage of producers and the studio in depicting contemporary and often below-the-surface attitudes such as anti-Semitism in *Gentleman's Agreement* and *Pinky,* even at the risk of box office backlash.[14] Beyond the evaluative question of whether or not a film might have gone far enough in its exploration of the issues framing its story, critics lauded both films for creating a means to provoke needed thought and debate on important contemporary issues.[15] *Gentleman's Agreement* went on to win the Academy Award for Best Picture of 1947.

Speculation about the permanent impact of semidocumentary style on future Hollywood film production recurs in the reviews these films received. The opening of *Variety's* review of *13 Rue Madeleine* asserts that it "is the type of film which will become increasingly interesting and box-office-valuable the longer history removes us from World War II" (18 Dec. 1946: 14). In holding up *Northside* to "those who generalize too glibly about the superiority of European movies," *Time* argues that "if still better movies are going to be made in the U.S. as a habit rather than a rare miracle of fighting luck (e.g., *Treasure of Sierra Madre*), they will probably be made by extending—and transcending—this journalistic technique" (16 Feb. 1949: 99). In a similar vein, the *New Republic* values the documentary technique of *Boomerang!* over the distractions it had seen two weeks earlier in *Lady of the Lake*.[16] In reviewing *Boomerang!*, *Newsweek* notes the upcoming *Northside* and attributes the current location work in *The Kiss of Death* and *Miracle on 34th Street* specifically to Zanuck's push away from studio shooting.[17] *Time* felt that in *Boomerang!*, "an important corner is turned, away from Hollywood's rather monotonous dreamland, into the illimitable possibilities of the world the eye actually sees. Around that corner, many other films may follow, to everybody's profit" (10 Mar. 1947: 97).

Hortense Powdermaker lauded films that dared to break the rules and deliver "messages" in the mid-1940s as both innovative and appropriate in addressing the concerns of their audiences. Powdermaker cites a survey of individual film viewers by a writer/producer who found that above all else audiences wanted "honest" pictures (46). By addressing contemporary social issues, films such as *Crossfire, Lost Weekend,* and *Pinky* broke the cycles of imitation inherent within the "dream factory's" production system. They appealed to audiences that had become more demographically diverse and better educated, in part because of an increase in higher education after World War II (45). She notes that *Pinky, Home of the Brave,* and *Lost Boundaries* were all commercially "successful in the South" despite fears they would fail (40–41).

James Agee applied comparable critical values in reaching similar conclusions in his film reviews published in the *Nation* throughout the 1940s. Agee appreciated the journalistic strength a topical film gained through location shooting. *Boomerang!*, for example, was "a work of journalistic art" (289). In his review of *Kiss of Death*, Agee noted that the film

> illustrates a new and vigorous trend in U.S. moviemaking. One of the best things that is happening in Hollywood is the tendency to move out of the place—to base fictional pictures on fact, and, more importantly, to shoot them not in painted studio sets but in actual places. (376)

Location shooting improves filmmaking both technically and dramatically because

> if good technicians pay careful attention to the actual world, they can hardly help turning out a movie that is worth seeing; and the actors who have to play up to this world are greatly stimulated and improved by their surroundings, too. (275)

Agee saw the direction of future innovation in the semidocumentary style evident in *House, Rue, Northside,* and *Boomerang:*

It is hard to believe that absolutely first-rate works of art can ever again be made in Hollywood, but it would be idiotic to assume that flatly. If they are to be made there, they will most probably develop along the directions worked out during the past year or two; they will be journalistic, semi-documentary, and "social-minded," or will start that way and transcend those levels. (289–90)

The Hathaway Trilogy as Docudrama

The critical reception of these films points repeatedly to their effectiveness as docudrama. Since the three Hathaway works are drawn directly from actual events, they exemplify straightforwardly the defining characteristics of docudramatic argument. First, *House, Rue,* and *Northside* prominently foreground their documentary connections; second, the films build their narratives through melodramatic structures that argue for a moral affirmation reviews of the films suggest was valuable to the postwar audience;[18] and third, the films employ warranting strategies in their arguments for a melodramatic view such that their stories, and the moral positions that result, benefit from their close connection to the actuality claims on which the films are based.

The Hathaway films maintain explicit documentary connections. From the outset, each of these films claims its origin in previous texts that have an important basis in actuality. *House* and *Rue* explain their sources in government documents, cases contained in U.S. Army and domestic intelligence agency files, respectively. Their specific narrative lines have been gleaned from some number of these actual cases. *Northside,* on the other hand, was based on the specific story of Frank Majcek, whose conviction for murder was documented first in the Chicago *Times,* and then picked up by subsequent articles in *Time* (15 Aug. 1945) and *Reader's Digest* (Dec. 1946).

The films each assert actuality claims in their opening credits. These sequences are almost identical to each other in the kind and order of information they provide, as well as in their graphic strategies. In each case, the credits appear as typed text on white typing paper. *Rue* sets its credits up within a document folder suggesting a case file titled "13 Rue Madeleine"; *Northside's* opening title adds a hand that comes on-screen to stamp "URGENT" on the cover of its file folder. After the screen credits, all three films have explanatory titles that refer to the cases the films have been based on and state that the films were shot on the actual locations of these events "whenever possible." *Northside's* further makes a straightforward statement that "this is a true story."[19]

All three films have titles (addresses and a telephone number) that identify a precise location. This initial link of story and geographic specificity is further reinforced by the first sequences in each film after the opening credits. All of these show stock footage of the "actual locations" where the films will "whenever possible" be set. As the stories' characters appear, re-created locations are sequenced with actual locations to underscore the documentary basis of these images.

The sense of close connection to documentary actuality is furthered by a tendency to favor images of documents. Documents appear and function like characters. As espionage films, *Rue* and *House* cast crucial documents in starring roles.[20] *Rue* begins with shots of case folders in army filing cabinets. Close-ups of identity documents factor into depicting the selection and training of new agents and appear even more prominently later, when the Gestapo's examination of a hotel registry threatens to expose James Cagney's Bob Sharkey, who is undercover in occupied France and highly vulnerable. Newly recruited agents are taught with actual military aircraft identification film as part of their training. When *Northside* has James Stewart's J. P. MacNeal surreptitiously use a spy camera to photograph a police ledger, we see the page he is documenting through the camera viewfinder (see fig. 5). The recurrence of images of photographs and printed words may simply hark back to Hathaway's origins as a silent film director. The iconography nonetheless frames and privileges text. The frequent interaction of character and photographic document reasserts the claimed proximity to actuality.

Through the blending of elements of narrative and documentary form, documentary material is shaped melodramatically in all three narratives. Each film displays some fundamental characteristics of domestic melodrama. Literal or figurative families struggle within powerful, repressive social systems, with relatively powerful and powerless characters positioned accordingly. Narrative development functions in each case to argue for moral affirmation.

The melodramatic "curve" of the trilogy builds chronologically, with *Northside* the most overtly melodramatic film of the group. The espionage films center on spy groups that function as figurative families, with the leaders (Lloyd Nolan's Briggs in *House;* Cagney's Sharkey in *Rue*) depicted paternalistically. Cagney's right-hand man is even nicknamed "Pappy."[21] Within the larger, oppressive setting of the world war, *Rue* and *House* focus on the inner workings of opposed intelligence communities. In both films, this powerful, profoundly dangerous social system pivots around double agents.[22] While complex in plot, *Rue* and *House* are never uncertain morally. Cagney's death at the end of *Rue* (in a scene that closely recalls the interrogation scene near the conclusion of Rossellini's 1945 *Rome, Open City*) is necessary to spare him further torture and to prevent the Normandy invasion plans from becoming revealed. Dietrich, the main character, is wounded seriously at the end of *House,* also in the course of trying to prevent stolen information from reaching the wrong hands. The same moral system mandates the inevitable death of his opponents.

In the spirit of 1940s melodrama, both espionage films argue that the logical culmination of character vulnerability is necessary, willing self-sacrifice for the "right" cause. The strongest characters in these films place their country's interests ahead of their own. The premise that the films are based in actuality renders the morality of their sacrifices all the more imperative.

Call Northside 777

If *Northside* has been a relatively neglected film, it may be in part because of previous efforts by film scholars to classify the film as a film noir (Tuska 194; Hirsh 172–73). James Stewart plays James P. MacNeal, an investigative reporter who attempts to unearth the truth behind the fourteen-year-old murder conviction of Frank Wiecek (Richard Conte). While the film never plunges into Wiecek's point of view, it certainly is the stuff of noir. Wiecek has lived the nightmare of an innocent trapped wrongly behind bars by an uncaring, corrupt legal system.[23] Stewart's investigation as reporter-turned-detective leads him to become immersed in the seamy underside of the city as well as the inner workings of a possible police conspiracy to keep the truth hidden.

Beneath this noirish surface, however, beats the heart of a melodrama. Rather than build on and eventually end with unresolved problems of moral uncertainty, *Northside* works to affirm the system of public knowledge that mistakenly convicts and then eventually frees Wiecek (Telotte 63). The film's affirmation of social order is entirely contrary to the pessimism characteristic of film noir. Functioning as a melodrama, the narrative restores the disruption of order and morality in the world of the film.

Furthermore, the narrative foregrounds basic melodramatic configurations. Literal and figurative families form a core of character interactions. Tillie Wiecek, Frank's mother, provides the catalyst for the narrative by running the classified advertisement that catches the attention of MacNeal's editor. She stands by her son, laboring as a scrubwoman during the decade and a half of his imprisonment to earn the money she hopes will fund his exoneration and release. For his part, Wiecek would rather remain in prison than have publicity that might help his case jeopardize his former wife's new life.[24] Wiecek's integrity only emphasizes his status as an innocent victim of an oppressively powerful (and fallible) legal system. Ultimately, MacNeal provides last-minute, photographic proof of his innocence, appropriately enough through documentation gleaned from a newspaper front page. MacNeal succeeds in saving Wiecek with the very weight of apparent fact that all along has victimized him.

Northside displays certain features of film noir within the narrative structure of a melodrama because the film is a docudrama, blending realistic atmosphere, detail, and story line in order to argue that the actual case was very much like the film that has resulted. As one of the films in TCF's social problem cycle, *Northside* illustrates the rhetorical strategies employed in the contemporary docudramatization of actuality. Like contemporary docudrama, *Northside*'s larger moral arguments draw strength from the film's claimed proximity to actuality. *Northside* favors images of printed material, actual locations, and actual technologies as actuality "anchors" to link directly the fictional and nonfictional elements of the film. This iconography shows how the basic docudrama warrants of models, sequences, and interactions are at work in substantiating the larger moral claims the film advocates.

Models in *Northside*

Images of printed documents pervade *Northside,* as they do *House* and *13 Rue.* These images not only refer to the original, actual documents that motivated the production of the films but also wield the force of expression turned to print. Their credibility claims in *Northside* stem from the implication that they are modeled on the original classified advertisement and the subsequent published stories that the film is now re-creating.

An extra-large close-up of Tillie's ad, circled by Kelly's copyediting marker, recurs in the film as it is shown first to MacNeal and then, subsequently, by MacNeal to those he interviews (see fig. 6) The same shot is also used in the trailers for the film, reiterating the links between re-creation, publicity, audience knowledge, and prior texts.

MacNeal's series of resulting stories also link previous, known, external texts to the film's internal narrative development. Throughout the film, we see MacNeal typing the stories that will become the paper's campaign to free Wiecek, beginning with his interviews with Tillie, Frank, and Helen. After Frank passes a lie detector test, the stakes increase. The stories detail police corruption and the search for Wanda Skutnick (the key witness), and ultimately brand Wanda a liar.

The visual pattern of these modeled images also connects dramatic content to printed expression. Drama unfolds in an interview; the thrust of the interview becomes the lead to the text of MacNeal's story as we see keys of the typewriter striking paper; MacNeal's words ultimately become a printed headline, the newspaper itself a part of the press run. Images of news in the film, then, function not only to narrate the melodramatic development of MacNeal's crusade but also to anchor the filmic drama to the external actuality of the prior texts the film has adapted.

In *Northside*'s modeling of actuality, images, scenes, and sequences resemble their original referents. Modeling is strictly iconic, its validity depending (as with any model) on the degree to which analogies exist between signified (original, actual subject matter) and signifier (its cinematic re-creation). Models entirely re-create people, places, actions, and events, approximating to some degree the "look" of the known. This strategy invites the viewer's collaboration by asking acceptance of the very premise that its re-creation comes "close" to the original.

Modeled material persuades as it situates its viewer as a collaborator in pretense. If we accept the resemblance to original appearance, beginning, in this instance, with Tillie Majcek's original advertisement, then we are that much more likely to accept the film's view of historical and moral truth. History entails morality. The model, as a model, sets up the validity of the larger moral argument of the film.

Sequences

The beginning of *Northside* sequentially links space in actual footage to re-created space. The re-creation resembles the original closely enough to generate spatial unity between the actual and re-created components of the sequence.

Northside opens with a montage of an aerial re-creation of the Chicago fire, stock footage of the city skyline, newspaper buildings, and newspaper headlines that segue into prohibition newsreel footage (of Capone and Dillinger and of a raided bootlegging operation). The film's voice-over narrator connects the setting, violence, the city's newspapers that document that violence, and the events about to unfold, using Sandbergesque language to evoke a sense of Chicago's toughness ("a city of brick and brawn, concrete and guts, with a short history of violence beating in its pulse"). The newsreel footage cuts to a shot of a city street corner, framing a policeman and a woman fighting the wind; this dissolves to the opening "proper" of the story, exterior views of Wanda's Grocery, and begins a longer scene re-creating the murder of a beat cop that will result in the incarceration of Frank Wiecek.

The murder scene dissolves to another headline announcing the crime; like the prior headline montage, this also dissolves into newsreel footage the narrator describes as the arrest of a bootlegger/informant. More newsreel shots of a raid on an apartment cut to an identical, re-created exterior of the apartment stairway that shows police taking in Frank and Helen Wiecek.

These sequences link efficiently *Northside*'s specific fictionalized story to immediate historical, geographical, and cultural contexts (gangsters and prohibition-era current events) as well as to elemental myths about Chicago ("brawn"; wind and fire; journalism, and the newsreel tradition of storytelling). Along with the overt claims to credibility stemming from the journalistic elements of this introduction to Frank Wiecek's story, there is an association of geographical and narrative veracity. The sequencing of actual and then re-created locations argues that if the scenes referred to appeared "like this," then other events also happened "this way." Geographical credibility argues for credibility of depicted action.

In *Northside*'s sequencing, when actual, indexical footage alternates with re-creation, the modeling of the iconic material is "tested" and its validity reinforced through its proximity to indexical imagery. It literally can "stand up" next to the "real" thing.

Docudrama sequencing also lends modeled materials an indexical presence, a kind of truth by association. If models are strictly iconic, arguing for proximity by virtue of resemblance to their actual referents, sequencing relations establish a more literal proximity when indexical footage alternates with re-created scenes.

Interactions

Since *Northside* tells such a specifically "Chicago"-rooted story, it made sense to shoot the film on location in and around the city. Several day and night location sequences show MacNeal searching Polish neighborhoods for Wanda Skutnick, eventually confronting her in her own bedroom. The search takes MacNeal to a series of bars and uncooperative interviews; the dark stairs and hallway leading to Wanda's apartment strike the closest chords to film noir in the entire film (see fig. 7).

The interaction of actor/character and actual location occurs throughout the film. The vast space of the state penitentiary cell block is echoed more subtly when MacNeal interviews Wiecek in the warden's office, and inmates are visible through the windows moving across a courtyard in the distant background, while the breeze rustles the awnings outside. Shots such as this continue the film opening's association of location realism with narrative credibility. Location authenticity also underlines melodramatic components of the film; when MacNeal first interviews Tillie Wiecek, Frank's mother, he finds her after hours, still scrubbing stairs in the empty, cavernous space of an office building. The time and place of the setting reinforce her claims to be working to free her son, and to have done so for over a dozen years.

The film hinges two of its most important sequences on interaction of character with props, specifically the "cutting edge" technology that will allow journalism to aid justice. Along with the more general functions of location, these scenes link the film's fictional constructions to extra-filmic, indexical resonances.

After some effort to arrange the test, MacNeal finally watches while Frank submits to a lie detector. Glance/object editing distributes our attention equally to tight shots of the lie detector apparatus, and looser shots of the technician who is explaining each step of the process to Wiecek, to Stewart, and to us. The technician's explanation is a performance equivalent to the grainy, faster film stock that so often signals "document"; his appearance and actions convey that he is a real-life lie detector administrator, drafted (and grafted) into this particular sequence to emphasize the reality of the story. A similar interaction sets up the film's climax. MacNeal and the pardon board await a wire transmission of an enlargement of a front-page news photo that will discredit the most damaging testimony against Wiecek. The blending of profilmic actuality with fictional characters helps imbue these moments with a documentary presence.

This kind of interaction draws upon both modeling and sequencing. Interaction in *Northside* and other docudramas establishes iconic and indexical proximity within the image, bringing actuality into the same cinematic space with the film's fictional constructions. Re-creation becomes strengthened by means of its copresence with actual material.

All three kinds of warrants describe types of proximities between the iconic and indexical signs that form a docudrama. Several further implications arise of modeling, sequencing, and interaction as warranting strategies. Warrants can be interdependent. Sequencing relies upon modeled material, and interaction incorporates both models and sequences. Proximity increases and therefore strengthens as strategies shift to the more complex relations of sequencing and interaction. As proximity strengthens, so does the warrant, therefore so does the apparent validity of the argument and ultimately the film's potential persuasive power.

As a melodrama, *Northside* bills itself as a story of a "mother's faith" and the journalistic courage that faith motivates. The film's narrative, dramatic, and photographic links to external actualities—the "actual story," the actual actors, the actual locations and props—warrant the film's melodramatic view, giving what would be otherwise "merely" melodrama a persuasive validity.

Warranting Processes in Recent Docudrama

The sense that *13 Rue Madeleine, The House on 92nd Street,* and *Call Northside 777* show us what "really happened" derives from warranting strategies that link documentary material and the clarity of melodramatic perspective. The key to any docudrama's retelling of history is its degree of closeness to the actual people, places, actions, and events that offer story material. All three kinds of warrants describe types of proximities between the iconic and indexical signs that form the film. In each case, proximity, the degree of closeness to actuality, validates the film's claim and affects the strength of its persuasive argument.

TCF's "semidocumentaries" provide a precedent for showing how the interrelationship of iconic and indexical material is crucial to the persuasive power of film docudrama. Contemporary docudrama depends upon the same interrelations to associate cinematic proximity (image resemblances; shot/scene sequencing; profilmic interactions) with the moral truth a film will advocate. Robert Redford's *Quiz Show* (1994) launches its view of the circumstances surrounding Charles Van Doren's notoriety from the premise that its re-creation of, for example, the image of Van Doren encased in a glass booth, or his testimony before a Congressional subcommittee, will be acceptable to audiences with primary memories, as well as those with only secondary familiarity with the original events. Films as different as Steven Spielberg's *Schindler's List* (1993) and Penny Marshall's *A League of Their Own* (1992) exploit the proximity of interactions in their concluding sequences. In all cases, the documentary appearance of the actual subjects of the stories we have just seen draws together the original and its re-creation, signified and signifier, allowing the latter to confirm the former through its very appearance.

Redford's *Quiz Show* demonstrates how resemblance can be made morally persuasive. General and broadcast histories offer a well-documented sense of what happened in the 1950s TV quiz show scandals, who the major players were, and how their public images were established and shifted as events evolved.[25] In this view, the quiz show scandal in general and the case of Charles Van Doren in particular reveal a moral weakness in the American social fabric, exposing a willingness to compromise intellectual integrity and public trust for the sake of celebrity and material gain.[26] The film re-creates this chapter in the history of television, however, to deliver an even more particularly focused moral argument: The source of the scandal was contestant, network, and sponsor greed, ignited by an incendiary spark of anti-Semitism. Charles Van Doren was brought down by his own social and intellectual elitism. Based on Richard N. Goodwin's account of the scandal and its investigation, *Quiz Show* depicts the known event framework, re-creating the established images these people and events entail, and then building onto this more personal and speculative material.

Consistent with preexisting accounts, the film shows Van Doren replacing Herbert Stempel as a contestant on *Twenty-one*. Stempel's anger at the dismissive treatment he receives leads to the charges he brings publicly, contributing to the subsequent series of investigations, first by a New York grand jury, then by a House of Representatives special subcommittee on legislative oversight.[27] The film departs from the general tenor of printed accounts and establishes a more unique perspective by underlining Stempel's Jewishness and his claims of anti-Semitism in the rigging of the shows.[28] The film's characterization of Stempel consistently foregrounds his ethnicity. One of the show's producers calls Stempel "an annoying Jewish guy with a sidewall haircut." When Stempel reveals to his family that he has been ordered to lose, he says viewers of that night's show will get to see Charles Van Doren "eat his first Kosher meal." Class and ethnic similarities and differences between Stempel, Van Doren, and Goodwin emerge strikingly in subsequent scenes. Goodwin interviews Stempel in his Bronx apartment. Toby, Stempel's wife, hair in curlers, blouse unbuttoned, and in the middle of inhaling nasal spray, leaps from her overstuffed chair as Herb admits Goodwin to their living room. She hustles out to serve coffee and *rugullah,* a pastry Goodwin "knows." Stempel asks Goodwin how a guy "like him" was able to get into Harvard. He asserts that the fix is anti-Semitic, that "a Jew is always followed by a gentile, and the gentile always wins more," a charge that Goodwin later confirms. By way of contrast, in the next scene, Goodwin visits the Van Dorens at their Connecticut estate. He walks past Charlie's brand-new, red Mercedes convertible and sits down to a family picnic lunch with Edmund "Bunny" Wilson, Thomas Merton, and a flock of Van Dorens. The gossip is about how one of the aunts had an affair with Wendell Wilkie.

Quiz Show further departs from established historical accounts by asserting that Van Doren was, in fact, intellectually and visually comparable to the scandal's primary investigator. Scenes scrupulously give "Charlie" and "Rick" equal visual weight as they test each other. During a lunch at the Athenaeum Club (Van Doren orders a Waldorf salad, Goodwin the Reuben), an exchange of similarly composed close-ups shows that Goodwin refuses to be intimidated by Mark Van Doren, Charlie's famous father, in pointing out the ethnically segregated nature of the clientele. The film employs a similar cinematically dramatic strategy during a poker game, when Charlie and Rick confront each other about "lying" and "bluffing." Reinforcement of the visual equality of investigator and the one investigated also occurs when Goodwin reluctantly must serve Van Doren with a subpoena to appear before the House subcommittee. The leading two-shot shows both men to be dressed almost identically as they walk and discuss how they've come to be on opposite sides of legal and moral issues stemming from the choice of wealth and fame, on the one hand, and retaining one's integrity, on the other (see fig. 8).

Through its cinematic presentation of Van Doren and Goodwin, *Quiz Show* adds a broader set of arguments regarding the implicit anti-Semitism in the network's actions to the re-creation of known history, the corruption and greed underlying the scandal. The proximity of re-creation warrants the film's moral position. From the premise of the "look" of the time, setting, characters, and actions, the film argues that Van Doren's downfall results from a double moral weakness. His cloistered office, family home, and upper-class Eastern family life can't shield him from being exposed as a cheater. Perhaps worse, however, is that he would allow himself to benefit from and then be ruined by the anti-Semitism of others, a prejudice, his friendship with Rick Goodwin would suggest, he himself does not necessarily share.

The action of *Quiz Show*'s arguments, its infusion of a particular moral view into re-creating documented history, illustrates the most basic issue raised by modeling relations in docudrama. Modeled warrants are entirely iconic and function by virtue of resemblance to their referents. The first question these warrants raise then becomes, understandably, "resemblance to what?" *Quiz Show*'s arguments suggest that resemblances to people and setting in modeled docudrama propose a more limited, clearly defined set of claims than depicted resemblances to actions and events. The second set of appearances, dependent upon the first, will then be more likely to raise ethical implications of historical representation.

Sequencing and interaction relations give modeled materials an indexical presence, implying truth by association. While models argue for proximity as they resemble their actual referents, sequencing and interaction relations create more literal proximities because indexical footage alternates with re-creation.

Similar examples of these strategies at work occur at the conclusions of two very different films, Penny Marshall's *A League of Their Own* (1992) and Spielberg's *Schindler's List*. The actual subjects of each film participate in epilogic action. Geena Davis's Dottie Hinson watches the ballplayers portrayed in *League* playing baseball now, as the older women they've become. Surviving former Schindler Jews in turn place stones on Oskar Schindler's grave in Jerusalem, escorted by the actor or actress who portrayed them in the film we've just seen. Both concluding sequences fulfill a grounding function. They convert the earlier models each film has offered from iconic abstractions to indexically based validations of the larger moral arguments the films are forwarding. Despite the differences in the two films, there are striking similarities in the way their conclusions depend upon these warrants to function. The conclusions are comparable in their time frames, numbers of characters involved, and actions portrayed.

First, both epilogues offer present-day documentary footage. The shift out of the fictional portrayal of a character as s/he may have existed in the past to an indexical image of that person in the film's present infuses their image (and the narrative that has preceded) with a more than fictional, extra-filmic presence. The women of *League,* despite their age, are still at it, playing ball, reinforcing how the film has asserted the importance of their love of the game, and a larger notion that the accomplishments in breaking gender barriers the film portrays ought to be recognized. The *Schindler* actors appear as such, out of costume, makeup, and character, in effect doubling the tribute their real-life counterparts are paying to the film's main character. The shift from past/fiction to present/actuality asserts that the films' positions toward their subjects possess an extra-filmic, enduring validity.

Both sequences feature groups. The large numbers of bodies on screen testify to the degrees of moral truth the films argue for; if this many people are actually involved, we are offered a confirmation by consensus.

The groups we see, moreover, are involved in rituals that affirm the significance of the experiences these stories document. The stones accumulating on Schindler's tombstone, like the quick shots showing the current abilities of the former ballplayers to catch, throw, and run, suggest that the action of the group remains greater than its individual parts. Ball playing and the honoring of the dead demonstrate ritualistically the endurance of group action, and its importance for a larger society. The different rituals share common ideological functions in that for both films, the reality of the group and its persistence into present day offer a final argument for social optimism: What is important will last, will be remembered, will provide grounds for understanding, possibly even unity, and ultimately the world will be better for it.

The sense that past as well as recent docudramas such as *Quiz Show* and *A League of Their Own* allow us to see what "really happened" derives from warranting strategies that link documentary material and melodramatic perspective. The next two chapters will consider how the very fusion of document and melodrama raises concerns about the value of docudrama as history, and the ethical implications of viewing the real through the emotional logic narrative form encourages. Docudrama offers a compelling kind of reasoning because the cues that signal that models, sequences, and interactions have shown us a logical path from actual premise to melodramatic conclusion set up an almost purely cinematic process of persuasion, a spatial association of what was "there" with the sense the film suggests we make of it. Docudrama warrants employ strategies based upon perceived proximities so that docudrama, at its most powerful, convinces us that it is properly both logical and emotional to associate cinematic proximity with moral truth.

3 | Dramatic Evidence: Docudrama and Historical Representation

D
ocudrama's recurrence on large and small screens suggests that the mode potentially can have a significant impact on historical discourse. The relationship between documentary and docudrama, however, raises reasons to preclude docudrama from the arena of historical debate. For their part, historiographers see the impact of the dramatic re-creation of the past as an ongoing issue in presenting thinking about actual events.[1] Re-created and narrated views of history provide a logical, often necessary, basis for the exchange of ideas. This chapter will consider the influence of docudrama on the view of history it represents. One of Twentieth Century-Fox's "semidocumentaries," *13 Rue Madeleine,* which was discussed in the last chapter, shows how docudrama's tendency to personalize history leads to the portrayal of the duration of historical time through pivotal moments.

Docudrama and Document

By definition, docudrama is not documentary, so the validity of its view of history, its "cash value" for its audience, remains problematic. Chapter 1 noted how one of the strongest voices addressing the issues raised by comparing dramatic and documentary representation in film belongs to Bill Nichols. Nichols systematically takes the position that telling stories and representing history are fundamentally distinct tasks. This chapter will show, however, that historiographers consider the work of writing history largely to be storytelling. As a documentary theorist, Nichols makes throughout his work an unmitigating distinction between documentary's direct roots in reality and the more metaphorical view of actuality that stems from narrative re-creation.[2] In *Blurred Boundaries* (1994), he further considers the epistemological implications of the re-creation of actuality in "reality TV" forms.

In his earlier book, *Representing Reality* (1991), Nichols argued that documentary is nonnarrative and documentarists "share a common, self-chosen mandate to represent the historical world rather than imaginary ones" (14). As a result, documentary works belong to the "discourses of sobriety" (5) that represent "the" world rather than "a" world (112). Documentaries tell us directly about "the" world in which we live. Fictional representations, on the other hand, offer us a "metaphoric relationship to history and lived experience" (5), and are not documents. Documentary presents a rooted discourse: "We prepare ourselves not to comprehend a story but to grasp an argument. We do so in relation to sounds and images that retain a distinct bond to the world we all share" (5). The logic of a film's argument begins with the documentary solidity of its evidence. Documentary allows argument because it presents "facts" by bringing us into direct contact with the historical world:

> The viewer then sets out to process the film with an understanding that the metaphorical distance from historical reality established from the outset by fiction . . . has been closed. . . . The text presents a metonymic representation of the world as we know it (the sounds and images bear a relation of part to whole; they partake of the same order of reality as that to which they refer) rather than a metaphorical rendering (where the images and sounds operate on a separate and distinct plane of resemblance to the historical world). Where fiction achieves a "reality effect" by sprinkling doses of authentic historical references across the realm of its creation—costumes, tools, vehicles, known places, or prominent figures—the same references within documentary serve as tangible evidence from the historical world in support of an argument. (28)

In the case of documentary re-creation, a viewer enters into what Nichols terms "a documentary mode of engagement" (25) in which a viewer is swayed more by logic of argument and evidence than by suspension of disbelief, or identification with a character (29–30).

Nichols acknowledges in *Representing Reality* the need for some documents to re-create their subjects, especially when the problematic accessibility of the truth warrants reconstruction:

> In most documentaries that include reconstructions, the reconstruction derives from historical, factual evidence, as in *Night Mail* and *The War Game.* The premise that historical evidence backs them up also lends plausibility to the subjective reenactments in [other] films. . . . [Errol] Morris, however, ignores the conceit that allows the documentarist to reconstruct the mise en scene of presumed truth. The "truth" in this case is far more elusive, shrouded by time but even more by memory, desire, and the logical paradox that it is impossible for any statement to vouchsafe its own truth status. (100)

In this warranted kind of re-creation, Nichols allows that proximity to evidence signals allegiance to "the" world rather than "a" world.

Blurred Boundaries questions the implications of the "blurs" between fiction and nonfiction forms (particularly those emerging from TV). Nichols's most basic concerns remain the validity of any assertions possible about the external, historical world when such mergers occur. In maintaining the distinction between documentary and fiction, Nichols extends the story/argument duality of *Representing Reality* to distinguish the authenticity of indexical evidence from the inventedness of narrative interpretation, a step necessitated by the marketing of "reality TV" products as actualities. The difference becomes even more critical when ostensibly nonfiction forms such as "reality TV" programs and even news broadcasts assume the strategies of narrative fiction.

At the core of Nichols's distinction between narrative and document remains his view of evidence and argument. Indexical evidence is "factual." Logical argument must reason from evidence. The indexical evidence presented in documentary functions "to authenticate the film's claims to represent some aspect of the historical world" (*Boundaries* 47). Authenticity of evidence and, consequently, validity of argument grow from this direct connection to lived experience. Narrative weakens this connection, rendering problematic the value of "facts" when presented in a narrative context:

> Inevitably, the distinction between fact and fiction blurs when claims about reality get cast as narratives. We enter a zone where the world put before us lies between one not our own and one that very well might be, between a world we may recognize as a fragment of our own and one that may seem fabricated from such fragments between indexical (authentic) signs of reality and cinematic (invented) interpretations of this reality. (ix)

Re-creation, by definition, is indexically linked to the present and cannot offer the same kind of authentic, primary evidence:

> Reenactments came to be denounced as fabrications in the days of observational cinema; then, more recently, filmmakers resurrected them as a legitimate way to address what is not available for representation in the here and now. But unlike the written account, the reenactment lies anchored, indexically, to a present distinct from the past it re-presents. The very authenticity of the image testifies to the use of source material from the present moment, not the past. This presents the threat of disembodiment; the camera records those we see on screen with indexical fidelity, but these figures are also ghosts or simulacra of others who have already acted out their parts. (4)

What reality TV and network news reenactments do feed is a desire to feel a sense of connectedness to the world. "We hunger for news from the world around us but desire it in the form of narratives, stories that make meaning, however tenuous, dramatic, compelling, or paranoid they might be" (ix). This feeling of connection comes from the simulation of the historical world. Consumption of reality TV products provides a sense of participation in a fictional kind of confessional.

> Reality TV offers communion drawn from atomized, dissociated figures who remain so; a sense of engagement, empathy, charity, and hope built on a disengaged, detached simulation of face-to-face encounter; and a sense of coherence and continuity, if not suspended animation, at a time when ideas and values feel worn, ineffective, abused, and bandied about. (56–57)

When "the historical world becomes reduced to a set of simulations and idle talk" (52), the result cannot be knowledge that provides a sound basis for sober discourse about the world. When simulation is subordinated within a traditional narrative structure, narrative hegemony fosters reception as detached consumption exactly the opposite of a more direct, Sartrian engagement with the external (53). Works that re-create reality can offer worthwhile historical discourse if they put readers on notice about the status of a text, and discourage unthinking, passive consumption. If reenactment is one strategy of presentation in a larger collaging of available materials, producing a self-conscious discourse that "suspends historical explanation" and allows a viewer to "fill in," to attain some "sense" of history as lived time, as "embodied knowledge," then a work fulfills the potentials of postmodernist history, one that allows validity of argument through honesty of presentation (146, 119–21).

In sum, Nichols's work develops three reasons to preclude nonindexical representations from the arena of historical discourse. First, re-created material allows a false sense of connectedness to the world. Second, recreation is indexically linked to the present, rather than the past it purports to represent. Third, given the nature of its "evidence," dramatic recreation can only interpret, rather than argue. It remains to consider each of these positions in relation to docudrama.

The problem of false connectedness results from conditions of reception. Much of *Blurred Boundaries* targets justifiably the potentially deceptive nature of fictions "passing" as fact. "Blurring" occurs on the level of reception because of the ready mix TV programming offers of nonfiction and fiction products.

By comparison, MOWs and docudramas exhibited in theaters as feature films present themselves as fictions based on actuality, clearly foregrounding the fact that they are stories. Docudramas avoid a major, potential deception of reality TV forms because their modes of presentation and the conditions of their reception emphasize their status as works of narrative fiction. What they may assert because they are "based on" fact is more problematic.

Chapter 1 proposed that a factual "basis" gives re-creation an indexical quality. The issue is critical in assessing the value of docudrama evidence. It would be this "evidence" that allows fact-based fictions validity as representations of history. In light of the absolute nature of Nichols's documentary/fiction distinction, a case needs to be made for how docudramas do qualify as arguments, and how they maintain a direct connection to their "real" referents in doing so.

Arguments by definition build logically from evidence to conclusion. The terms of Nichols's documentary/fiction duality (argument/story; evidence/reality effect; engagement/suspension of disbelief) rest squarely on the notion of the index, the sign of photographic "fact." Photographic evidence has a direct, motivated relationship to its referent, certainly a primary kind of evidence of history.

Re-created and reconstructed material may not be evidence possessing the same kind of "directness" as an on-the-spot photograph; however, re-creation by definition has a motivated relationship to the referent it re-creates. The closer it is to actuality, the more complete and the more effective it is as re-creation. In *Representing Reality,* Nichols acknowledged the validity of documentary reconstruction "derived" from "historical, factual evidence" (100). Truth becomes a matter of proximity. To pursue the issue further, photographic indexes are still selected, framed, focused, and filmed—that is, formulated—so that proximity to their actual referent is as much a factor for them as it is for re-creative significations.

For this reason, historian Robert Rosenstone questions the indexical element of documentary film evidence. Representation entails mediation, and consequently, "documentary is never a direct reflection of an outside reality, but a work consciously shaped into a narrative which—whether dealing with past or present—creates the meaning of the material being conveyed" (*Visions* 33). These considerations of form and mediation return us to the questions, Is an index an absolute kind of sign? Can indexical representation be partial? Is a photograph the same kind of index as a thermometer? Light striking a photographic emulsion may be directly analogous to temperature or air pressure driving mercury through a glass tube, but the photograph also derives from further manipulations (camera angle, height, and distance; film stock; lens selection; etc.). The photograph's iconic construction mediates the link between signifier and signified. Indexical signification, then, is a function of the degree of directness, the degree of motivation between signifier and signified.

If the quality of evidence in either documentary or docudrama stems from its directness, the nature of the link between signifier and signified, then so does the nature of the argument either kind of film might forward. Docudramas may argue hypothetically but still offer arguments based on evidence. Re-creation has its basis in historical reality, allowing a wide range of degrees of proximity to its original source. An argument in a docudrama based on re-created evidence is valid to the extent that it is modeled on the original referent(s). Docudrama, with its narrative form and evidence drawn from dramatic reconstruction, may not offer the "sober" discourse of a strictly nonfiction mode. The value of its advocacy, however, still deserves to be judged on the quality of its evidence and logic, rather than to be dismissed altogether from the arena of historical discourse because its consumption as narrative precludes its status as rhetoric.

Historiography and Docudrama

Historiographers Hayden White and Robert Rosenstone provide a useful basis for understanding how docudramas, like other historical narratives, construct their representations. Their different works share the position that any writing of history necessarily reformulates the primary experience of the time it documents. A key historiographic issue besides accuracy of representation becomes the honesty of the form of presentation.[3] In Rosenstone's and White's views of historiography, docudrama's lack of unmediated, direct presentation of facts does not preclude the mode from representing history and engaging in the discourse that debates relevant issues. To the contrary, both Rosenstone and White point out that narrative re-creation provides and structures much of what we understand history to be but carries with it the risk of emotion overshadowing reason. The question Nichols raises (can docudrama really argue?) becomes, What is the impact of its form on the argument that a docudrama makes?

White, like Nichols, begins with the basic distinction between real reports and fictions, suggesting that what will qualify as "history" has truth value because of its allegiance to the real. A work of history contributes to the "discourse of the real" (20). As White notes:

> The notion of what constitutes a real event turns, not on the distinction between true and false (which is a distinction that belongs to the order of discourses, not to the order of events), but rather on the distinction between real and imaginary (which belongs both to the order of events and to the order of discourses). One can produce an imaginary discourse about real events that may not be less "true" for being imaginary. (57)

Docudrama, with its balancing of reconstruction and invention, contributes to historical discourse to the extent that it has its basis in reality.

Directness of evidence is only one consideration in assessing historical discourse. Documentary offers one type of history but not the only kind. Rosenstone's reluctance to privilege documentary representation in comparing documentary and the historical film indicates the wide range of possible proximities between representation and referent.

The usefulness of a representation of history, in Hayden White's term, its "authority," only begins with its proximity to actuality, since "the authority of the historical narrative is the authority of reality itself; the historical account endows this reality with form" (20). The truth value of a narrative account of past events is a function of its closeness to those events, as well as the kind of sense it makes to us. "Both the facts in their particularity and the narrative account in its generality must meet a correspondence, as well as a coherence, criterion of truth value" (40).

Rosenstone agrees that storytelling does not preclude historical film from truth telling, and so from presenting history:

> At the outset, we must accept that film cannot be seen as a window onto the past. What happens on screen can never be more than an approximation of what was said and done in the past; what happens on screen does not depict, but rather points to, the events of the past. This means that it is necessary for us to learn to judge the ways in which, through invention, film summarizes vast amounts of data or symbolizes complexities that otherwise could not be shown. We must recognize that film will always include images that are at once invented and true; true in that they symbolize, condense, or summarize larger amounts of data; true in that they impart an overall meaning of the past that can be verified, documented, or reasonably argued. (*Visions* 71)

Rosenstone also distinguishes between true and false invention in storytelling. The former "engages the discourse of history," while the latter ignores that discourse (72). If actuality motivates its re-creation, then inventive representation will be based on the "truth."

The historical film employs the strategy of personalizing its stories.

Rosenstone describes the resulting "proximate fictions" as "small fictions used, at best, to create larger historical 'truths,' truths which can be judged only by examining the extent to which they engage the arguments and 'truths' of our existing historical knowledge on any given topic" (145). The historical film "has less to do with fact than with intensity and insight, perception and feeling, with showing how events affect individual lives, past and present. To express the meaning of the past, film creates proximate, appropriate characters, situations, images, and metaphors" (*Revisioning* 7). Accounting for events in a dramatic mode leads to an emphasis on character and human agency.

> The point: both dramatic features and documentaries put individuals in the forefront of the historical process. Which means that the solution of their personal problems tends to substitute itself for the solution of historical problems. More accurately, the personal becomes a way of avoiding the often difficult or insoluble social problems pointed out by the film. (*Visions* 57)

The emphasis on the personal, dramatic presentation of social concerns (rather than an analysis of issues as dedramatized abstractions) also allows for the framing of moral issues. White notes that the telling of history through stories renders it desirable, and ultimately leads historical representation to function morally. He explains:

> I merely wish to suggest that we can comprehend the appeal of historical discourse by recognizing the extent to which it makes the real desirable, makes the real into an object of desire, and does so by its imposition, upon events that are represented as real, of the formal coherency that stories possess. (20–21)

Docudrama, I will suggest below, also makes temporal duration desirable. Desirability presupposes preference, value, and the process of judgment, components of a moral system. Part of that desirability depends upon the type of proximity to the past a narrative account allows. White distinguishes between "narrating," storytelling that can be equivalent to journalistic reporting, and "narrativizing." It is the difference between "a discourse that openly adopts a perspective that looks out on the world and reports it and a discourse that feigns to make the world speak itself and speak itself as a story" (2). Enveloping a reader or viewer within the space of a narrative provides the opportunity for moral instruction. A "narrativizing discourse serves the purpose of moralizing judgments" (24) because it places events in an order of narrative priority, rather than following the form of a chronicle:

If every fully realized story, however we define that familiar but conceptually elusive entity, is a kind of allegory, points to a moral, or endows events, whether real or imaginary, with a significance that they do not possess as a mere sequence, then it seems possible to conclude that every historical narrative has as its latent or manifest purpose the desire to moralize the events of which it treats. (14)

Narrativizing human actions renders them meaningful in both experiential and moral terms. White refers to Paul Ricoeur's notion of "emplotment" to identify the moral implications of sequencing judgments that also convey a sense of the duration of the referent:

The meaning of stories is given in their "emplotment." By emplotment, a sequence of events is "configured" ("grasped together") in such a way as to represent "symbolically" what would otherwise be unutterable in language, namely, the ineluctably "aporetic" nature of the human experience of time. (173)

The validity of evidence that forms the basis for the representation of history is as much of concern as the sources of the power and appeal of its argument, a power that draws on its positioning of a reader/viewer to receive an authoritative, experientially compelling, and, at the same time, implicitly moralizing discourse.

The risk of re-creational historical storytelling becomes the foregrounding of emotion (rather than idea) characteristic of melodrama. Rosenstone elaborates the risks accordingly:

The substitution of certain overwrought forms of emotion for a deeper understanding of personal and social realities [*sic*]. A way of blinding ourselves to social, political, economic—even personal—analysis and understanding. Yet melodrama has been the dominant mode of the Hollywood historical film, thus a major source of criticism of the historical film. (*Visions* 240)

The admonition suggests that docudrama will be historically useful to the extent that it does not capitulate to its melodramatic elements. In posing the key question in terms of learning, Rosenstone returns to the fundamental issue of the value of docudramatic representation, noting that

whatever historical understanding the mainstream film can provide will be shaped and limited by the conventions of the closed story, the notion of progress, the emphasis on individuals, the single interpretation, the heightening of emotional states, the focus on surfaces.

These conventions mean that history on film will create a past different from the one provided by written history; indeed, they mean that history on film will always violate the norms of written history. To obtain the full benefits of the motion picture—dramatic story, character, look, emotional intensity, process—that is, to use film's power to the fullest, is to ensure alterations in the way we think of the past. The question then becomes: Do we learn anything worth learning by approaching the past through the conventions of the mainstream film (conventions that are, through the global influence of Hollywood, understood virtually everywhere in the world)? (65)

In sum, docudrama, as a form of historical film, can have historical value to the extent that it offers motivated, truthful invention, close proximations, and analogies and contributes constructively to the debate surrounding efforts to visualize and understand the past. In the next chapter, I will take up the problem of proximity again as it affects the perception of docudrama as an ethical mode of representing its subject matter. For now, the issue surrounding historical films generally—both narrated and narrativized—remains "how adequately they embody its ongoing issues and insert themselves into the ideas and debates surrounding a historical topic" (*Revisioning* 7).

Docudramatic History

The personalizing of history and the resulting dependence on melodrama counterbalance the proximity to actuality docudramatic reenactment and re-creation might attain. The tension inheres in the fusion of modes. Docudrama's representation of history poses problems of validity and appeal. The issues are intertwined, since much of the appeal of docudrama results from the way the form asserts the validity of its view.

The positions of both White and Rosenstone toward "narrativized" history indicate how docudrama works to make history accessible and appealing. The strategy of employing the classic Hollywood narrative mode privileges character desire. The larger social forces that oppose individual desires also become rendered in "personal" terms when the groups involved in conflicts become figured as families. Resolution of conflicts of desire highlights a larger, essentially melodramatic, moral scheme.

Most importantly, docudrama presents history by personalizing time, marking it as both desirable and moral.[4] Pivotal moments in its view of history tend to be those when group efforts hinge on the actions of key individuals at crucial times. We share the characters' desire for time. The historical importance of pivotal moments becomes accessible as "lived" time, but, even more, as time endured for a larger moral purpose. Docudrama reminds us that these are people and actions anchored in actuality. The sense of the real that underlies representation warrants the filmic reconstruction of time. The emphasis on the moment as moment infuses time as selected and rendered by the film with presence, marking that time as both historically and morally significant. The last chapter examined how Twentieth-Century Fox produced a cluster of actuality-based films after World War II that stand as prototypes of contemporary docudrama. One of these texts, *13 Rue Madeleine,* shows readily how docudrama formulates historical time and action.

13 Rue Madeleine and the Pivotal Moment Strategy

13 Rue Madeleine's links to actuality, its actuality indicators, provide the material to frame the film's rendering of key moments, its "personalizing" of historically significant time. These links are largely implicit and contextual, working in concert with the film's opening claim to employ actual location shooting "whenever possible." Indirect links between subject and story signal that there is some degree to which actuality has motivated re-creation. Indirect links can include explicit and/or implicit references to the historical event framework that contributes to the setting of the narrative (representation of time, place, and events); representation of the figures involved; and representation of dialogue and action. An indirect link means that actuality has probably motivated its representation in the film, and that representation amounts to informed speculation.

13 Rue's initial claim and the introductory stock footage pin the narrative events that will follow to geographic particulars and specific incidents. Stock shots include Washington, D.C., streets and buildings, and brief glimpses of Japanese and German nationals under restraint, being led through crowds and described by the voice-over narrator as foreign agents captured on U.S. soil (see fig. 9). The sequence suggests the credibility, by association, of the film's subsequent re-creations. The stock footage places geography and space on a par with action and events.

The opening establishes the espionage context that has motivated this particular story. Voice-over narration and close-ups of file cabinet drawers help detail the network of armed forces intelligence groups that operated during the war. Actual espionage activity contextualizes the subsequent composite invention and re-creation. The operation of one specific group will be this film's subject. We are shown in turn the group's demographic makeup and training, and we are confronted with the problem of moles and the basic disinformation strategy that structures the story. As the plot unfolds, it draws further on indirect links to established history, what Pierre Sorlin has termed "symbolic time."[5] Resistance groups (their leaders and operations), the V2 bombing threat, and the pending D-Day invasion outline the general, known event framework for the film's plot, establishing both time of setting and time available for action.

The links to geographic specificity and the critical nature of the actual events hanging in the balance of plot resolution act as the springs that drive the "clocks" winding out on the mortality of the film's main character, Sharkey (James Cagney). As Sharkey moves progressively closer to direct confrontation with his arch rival, Kunzel, and death, his time available to act out his desires (to fulfill his mission; to live) becomes limited by the actions of others. The effect of personalizing time is to increase its desirability. Along with this compression of available time, the interests of the groups Sharkey represents increase. Progressively more and more is at stake, depending on the outcomes of his action within clearly delineated time frames. What would function as otherwise conventional suspense mechanisms gain added significance because they are coded historically. As history is "personalized," fictional "personal" time inserts itself into extradiegetic historical process, increasing the accessibility of the significance of that moment of "real" time.

The film conveys its key moments through means both topical and spatial. The context of V2 bombing and pending invasion locates the importance of character actions in historical chronology and translates time as the character lives it into spatial terms. Sharkey's death nears as he is compelled both to create space (dig his own grave) and to wait while the space of the English Channel is crossed, first by radio waves, and then by Allied bombers. Consequently, the film's suspense mechanisms operate through events of clearly delineated spatial duration that foreground character mortality, as well as the implications the death of the character would have in the actual events framework.

Three scenes provide the countdown running out on Sharkey. Within a succession of time lines, he must link his identity with ideologically "proper" space; kidnap Duclois (the collaborator who has designed the layout of the V2 facilities threatening the invasion force); and withhold what he knows about the invasion plans from his torturers.

When Sharkey first meets the Resistance group he must work with, its members believe he is a German agent and force him, at gunpoint, to start digging a grave. The sequence spatializes time by showing the progressive size of the hole. As the grave nears the critical depth, he is given a temporary reprieve (see fig. 10). Now the rendering of critical duration spatializes time through the London/mainland shortwave radio link. If Sharkey can have the proper code included in that night's news broadcast from London, the Resistance group will believe his real identity. His message is radioed out. That night's group of personal announcements from London does not include the given code message (appropriately nothing less than "a lamb is ready for the slaughter"). Just as the Sten guns are cocked and raised, the London announcer interrupts the news and inserts the awaited statement.

The process of capturing Duclois and spiriting him out of the country leaves Sharkey's fate up to the pacing of the action of the enemy. Sharkey must take Duclois from his hotel room during a diversion, a fake partisan attack that distracts the German troops guarding him. With their effort to stop the plane that will convey Duclois over the channel, the same troops determine the amount of time left to Sharkey to complete his mission.

Each pivotal moment represents an increasingly critical intersection of character, action, and setting. The stakes increase as more lives hang in the balance. Had Sharkey been executed by the Resistance group, the repercussions of his death would have been limited. Getting Duclois out of the country means, at the least, the destruction of the rocket bomb sites in Belgium.

Sharkey's capture puts in jeopardy the Allied invasion plans. His colleagues know there is only a limited amount of time even he can withstand torture. The cross-channel spatialization of time now takes the form of the bombing raid that must destroy the Gestapo headquarters at 13 Rue Madeleine, where Kunzel is interrogating Sharkey, before the entire invasion force is put at risk.

Each of these moments brings Sharkey closer to his inevitable death, but more important, each moment entails progressively greater group interests, from espionage group to bomb targets to Allied interests in general. If the worth of one life can be measured in terms of sacrifice for a just cause, then "personalizing" history here means representing how one endures moments of mortal vulnerability for the sake of that cause. The strategies that represent this particular history make it accessible by rendering time as desirable and ultimately moral.

The presence of time in the film derives from its desirability and results in the moral coding of time. What gives time its presence? Why is this rendering of duration "desirable"? Temporal presence stems from its location, quantity, and quality. The location of plot time in an established, external chronology allows the film's audience to know more about what constitutes salient events than the film's characters can know. Plot events refer us to the larger value of time. The film's suspense mechanisms establish the problem of the quantity of time through the successive deadlines Sharkey faces. He needs more of it. In light of how little time he has, the quality of time centers on the issue of whether or not Sharkey's time is well spent. The duration of time becomes a function of the effort he must expend to overcome elements that deter his desire to complete the mission (convincing the Resistance group to believe him; getting past the several German soldiers that remain in Duclois's hotel; holding off Kunzel's troops to effect Duclois's transfer onto the plane). Each obstacle to effective action costs Sharkey time. The film structures Sharkey's self-sacrifice precisely as time well spent, imbuing his duration of time, its presence, with value, encoding it morally.

The same kind of structuring of temporal presence recurs in *House on 92nd Street* (German agents are prevented from leaving the United States with the secret of the atomic bomb) and *Call Northside 777* (a reporter gets crucial information to a pardon board in time to save an innocent man from a lifetime in jail). Because the suspense template foregrounds its links to well-known, extradiegetic events, the presentation of temporal duration encodes personally desirable time with larger moral significance.

Time itself becomes so desirable in these films that characters become secondary to the flow of events. The presentation of time erects a bridge from the primacy classic Hollywood film form allocates to individual desire and character psychology to a sense, mediated by character, of historical process. Sharkey's death throws into perspective both the event that has caused it (espionage) and the event that it "affects" (a successful invasion). Character functions ultimately to provide a means of access to the importance of this moment in historical time. Character may initiate a "personal" perspective of history, but like any perspective strategy, we are allowed literally to see through character and suspense conventions to gain an understanding of why this moment in history is truly "momentous."

In all three films in the Hathaway cycle, the linking of history to fictionally mediated characters and their desires allows actual, extradiegetic time to become desirable and, therefore, accessible. As docudrama represents past events in these films, warranted moral structures, moral perspectives with clear links to actuality, ultimately provide the presence as well as the coherence of history.

Docudrama offers an appealing representation of actuality because of its coherence. Its representation of history does not pretend to be documentary in nature. Its representation is potentially neither more nor less valid than other historical films. Its validity stems from its proximity to its subject. The next chapter will consider further how the judgment of a docudrama as an ethical work depends directly upon the factor of proximity, that is, how close the work is perceived to be to its referents.

The case of *13 Rue Madeleine* indicates how the classic Hollywood narrative film structure of docudrama personalizes the time and events that constitute history. Time as chronological framework and time as a process of duration becomes an object of desire for both character and audience. With its range of links to actuality, however, docudramatic time's prioritizing of events and actions both infuses time with presence and encodes the value of time. Viewed docudramatically, history appears dramatic, personal, accessible, and moral. All told, these sources of its coherence sharpen the appeal of docudrama as it represents and explains our actions in time.

Fig. 1. Claustrophobic pursuit, *In the Name of the Father*

Fig. 2. Confinement, *In the Name of the Father*

Fig. 3. Schindler's domestic space, *Schindler's List*

Fig. 4. Goeth's house, *Schindler's List*

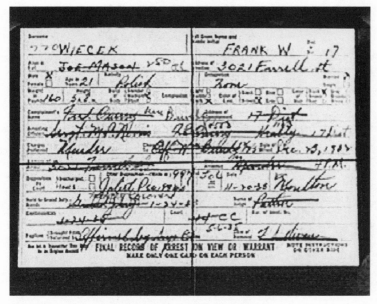

Fig. 5. Documents as costar, *Call Northside 777*

Fig. 6. Tillie's ad, *Call Northside 777*

Fig. 7. Location shooting, *Call Northside 777*

Fig. 8. Visual equality of friendly adversaries, *Quiz Show*

Fig. 9. Newsreel footage sequenced into *13 Rue Madeleine*

Fig. 10. Personal and historical time converging, *13 Rue Madeleine*

Fig. 11. Jim Garrison's investigators as family, *JFK*

Fig. 12. Garrison re-creating JFK's assassination, *JFK*

Fig. 13. Foregrounding media as document, *The Positively True Adventures of the Alleged Texas Cheerleader-Murdering Mom*

Fig. 14. Terry and Marla's domestic space, *The Positively True Adventures of the Alleged Texas Cheerleader-Murdering Mom*

Fig. 15. The Holloways' living room as the site of dreams, *The Positively True Adventures of the Alleged Texas Cheerleader-Murdering Mom*

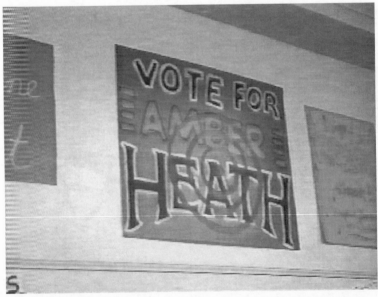

Fig. 16. Cheerleading turning lethal, *The Positively True Adventures of the Alleged Texas Cheerleader-Murdering Mom*

Fig. 17. Tony going Hollywood, *The Positively True Adventures of the Alleged Texas Cheerleader-Murdering Mom*

Fig. 18. Lefty's kitchen, *Donnie Brasco*

Fig. 19. Water as oppression, *Shine*

Fig. 20. Water as expression, *Shine*

Fig. 21. Brasco foiled by his own side, *Donnie Brasco*

Fig. 22. Beginning of *Rosewood*

Fig. 23. After the massacre, *Rosewood*

Fig. 24. Translation and agency, *Amistad*

Fig. 25. Nature bridging cultural difference, *Amistad*

Fig. 26. "Who we are is who we were . . . ," *Amistad*

Fig. 27. The price of ambition, *A Civil Action*

Fig. 28. Patch Adams's hearing as a community event, *Patch Adams*

Fig. 29. Coalwood residents watching the last launch, *October Sky*

Fig. 30. A Coalwood resident watching the last launch, *October Sky*

Fig. 31. Coalwood miners watching the last launch, *October Sky*

Fig. 32. Miss Riley watching the last launch, *October Sky*

Fig. 33. Homer's rocket gracing Miss Riley's sickbed, *October Sky*

4 | Docudrama Ethics and the Problem of Proximity

> [T]he dramatic power of dramadocumentary lies in its capacity to show us not that certain events occurred (the headlines can do that) or even, perhaps, why they occurred (for such information we can go to the weekly magazines or the history books) but *how* they occurred: how recognizable human beings rule, fight, judge, meet, negotiate, suppress, and overthrow.
> —David Edgar, "Theatre of Fact: A Dramatist's Viewpoint"

Early in his discussion of "dramadocumentary," David Edgar reviews some basic criticisms of the form. Dramatized documentary can intentionally or inadvertently deceive its audience. The willful distortion of known fact in order to create drama abuses history. Dramatized documentary also can become an opportunity to propagate political partisanship (175, 180). Edgar takes issue with these efforts to dismiss the legitimacy of the form; he compares, as do historiographers Hayden White and Robert Rosenstone, the advantages and shortcomings of dramatized documentary to other forms of history.

For Edgar, a basis in fact is what gives dramadocumentary, and by extension any account of history, its credibility (177). What a "fact" might be and what a "basis" might consist of in a re-creative form is not self-evident. Both point toward how the credibility of a docudrama's argument depends upon its proximity to its referents, its source material. The act of re-creation begins a series of ethical consequences, beginning with the very choice of subject to re-create. Subsequent decisions reveal the alignment, that is, the proximity, of actuality and re-creative representation. To develop further the notion of proximity, the cases of *JFK, Mississippi Burning,* and *The People Vs. Larry Flynt* will illustrate how docudramatic ethics become problematic when a work's relationship to its referents becomes an issue. The responses of critics to each film show where and how concerns arise: *JFK* makes creative additions to known source material; *Mississippi Burning* contradicts the historical significance of the events it depicts; and *The People Vs. Larry Flynt* omits known elements of its subject. Consequently, this sampling of cases suggests that unwarranted creative supplementation, contradiction, and omission of the known are fundamental kinds of ethical problems for docudrama, problems heightened by the ways docudrama re-creates known material within the narrative arc and the terms of reception audiences expect from fiction feature films.

JFK and the Ethics of Docudrama

As Oliver Stone's *JFK* exemplifies the indexical icons and the melodramatic configurations that form the defining characteristics of docudrama, it also sheds light on ethical considerations this mode of filmmaking raises. Melodrama forwards clear moral positions. *JFK* functions melodramatically in its efforts to wrest order from the chaos created by John F. Kennedy's assassination. Its "creative use" of actual materials in fact creates a melodramatic search for a moral order. In doing so, perhaps no other recent feature film docudrama has been as controversial, particularly regarding issues of the film's credibility, the accuracy of its re-creations, and the resulting validity of its view of its subject.[1] The case of *JFK* illustrates how ethical problems arise when docudrama steps too far from known, actual events into the realm of speculation. Ironically, *JFK* contains more actual "documentary" material than any of the other films considered here, a fact that fuels the charges of irresponsibility brought against film and filmmaker by a wide range of writers and critics.[2]

Melodrama becomes fused with documentary as *JFK* references well-known actual events and texts about those events in its focus on a key individual's struggle against powerful, corrupt forces of social control. Family structures background New Orleans District Attorney Jim Garrison's investigation into the Kennedy assassination. Garrison's work plays (in the film's view, selflessly) against his literal family, his wife, children, and their home life. We see his investigation as the function of a more figurative family, the group of assistants who share the investigative chores. The seed that grows into the investigation takes root in Garrison's family room while television news covers the funeral: Mrs. Garrison tries to pull her husband away from the screen and back into family matters, in what becomes a recurring tension between work and family. When the film shows Garrison with his team, they are often in "family" circle configurations, grouped around a table at a restaurant or in a living-room-like conference setting, the figurative father Garrison at the head (see fig. 11).

The implicit family context of Garrison's work is a secondary melodramatic configuration compared to the work itself. Garrison is launching nothing less than a search for order within a social system the investigation finds is far more chaotic and destructive than surface appearance suggests. The murder of the president and the underlying conspiracy Garrison uncovers at the highest levels of the federal government reveal the desacralized nature of the world of the film.

JFK presents itself as a film with a mission. The need to bring to public light *JFK*'s view of this conspiracy with its enormous, ongoing issues warrants the film's production. The fact of *JFK*'s widespread theatrical distribution (and its resulting controversy) argue that we should see this film, think about it, discuss it.

While *In The Name of the Father* is Gerry Conlon's story, and *Schindler's List* tells its audience about Oskar Schindler, *JFK* is not "about" JFK or even his death so much as it is "about" Jim Garrison. Unlike these other films, *JFK* does not bring a particular point of view to generally accepted facts about known events. Instead it attempts to build on the known to argue its theory. The film is a re-creation of several speculative, controversial works.

JFK raises ethical issues when it violates the warrants that allow docudramas to offer arguments by analogy. Is the film about a "deserving" subject? If Garrison's view of the Kennedy assassination has never received widespread acceptance, then why should this material warrant representation as a feature film docudrama? More particular charges against the film's distortions of "known" history—the Ferrie "confession," for example, before he is found dead[3] or the fabrication of "X" in order to validate the same kind of conspiracy charges—arguably result from the effort to bolster the warrant (the Garrison view is valuable to the film's audience and society generally) and inevitably jeopardize the film's entire argument.

If the first level of warranting has been thrown into question (that this story deserves to be told), then the second level of warranting must also be questionable (that the story must be told "this" way, through re-creation); however, it is generally agreed that if nothing else, *JFK* overwhelms its viewer with its interplay between actual and re-created materials.[4] Janet Maslin argues that the systematic, near-indistinguishable interplay of real and re-created footage ultimately confuses what is real and what is fictional.[5] Technical proficiency won't make for effective argument if the evidence can't be trusted.

What the film attempts to do, more specifically, is to re-create Garrison's speculations as he gathers evidence. A pattern of inferential thinking based on indexical material emerges from scene to scene in the film: Garrison is confronted with information, for example, from television news sources (early on), or through his associates reviewing gathered evidence (as the investigation gathers steam). While Garrison stands at a scene, such as the window of the third floor of the Texas School Book Depository or David Ferrie's cluttered apartment, the narration of events becomes illustrated by quickly flashed images, some actual (fragments of the Zapruder film as they discuss the progress of the limousine turning from Houston onto Elm) but more often than not re-created (staged, black-and-white images of other assassins standing at the stockade fence, of Oswald in the Dallas jail, of the murder of Ferrie, etc.) (see fig. 12). Garrison is thus "getting the picture," formulating an increasingly coherent view of complex fragments that will add up to an explanation of who did what, when, and why. If the speculation has persuasive power, it is because of the re-created material's proximity (both in place and resemblance) to the actual.

Objections to this strategy of sometimes shot-by-shot interplay of re-created and actual material have centered on the potential to mistake document for docudrama. Those most critical of the film charge it with blurring the distinction between historical fact and dramatic embellishment. The vast amount of actual and actual-looking images in *JFK* fuels what amounts to a critical backfire: Since it's such an "analogic"-looking docudrama, it offers a potentially powerful, persuasive view of its subject; however, by the same token, its departures from argument through literal analogies (close resemblances) as it develops its conspiracy theory render it susceptible to charges of irresponsibility.

In sum, concerns over *JFK*'s ethics understandably stem from its choice of subject (does Jim Garrison's conspiracy theory deserve to be told?) as well as its methods of re-creation (when does re-creation stop and imaginative speculation begin?). The interplay between indexical and indexically iconic materials in *JFK* takes to an extreme the mix of cues characteristic of docudrama as a mode: Documentary subject matter and materials appear embedded within a fiction narrative, communicated within a fiction feature film context (including theatrical distribution and exhibition); also, the fusion of documentary and narrative stylistics has a rhetorical objective easily confused with a literal claim to historical truth.

Mississippi Burning

If *JFK* risks violating the terms of its artistic license by creating events and figures many critics felt were unwarranted by the known history, *Mississippi Burning* raises concerns by virtue not of what it adds so much as what it poses that runs in direct contradiction to the known. *Mississippi Burning* was released in 1988, shortly after films such as *Missing* (1982), *Silkwood* (1983), and *The Killing Fields* (1984) helped foreground social concerns for 1980s feature film audiences, and just before the larger wave of early 1990s film and television docudramas. The film was director Alan Parker's second project after *Midnight Express* (1978) in which he adapted material based on actual events; consequently, critics again focused on how Parker would balance *Mississippi Burning's* presentation of political issues with its functions as entertainment (Davis 37). Patrick Rael put the film in the larger context of "freedom struggle films," films that

> are produced by the Hollywood movie establishment, but express an historical awareness of racial politics. Set in the Civil Rights Movement, the Civil War, or the struggle against apartheid, they constitute a film genre of considerable importance, for they are one of popular culture's rare attempts by whites to present entertainment politically sympathetic to blacks. (119)

Problems of contradiction arise, however, because of efforts to shape these works for and sell them to white audiences.

Critics of the film were concerned that *Mississippi Burning's* depiction of its subject, the murder of three civil rights workers in Mississippi in 1964, compromised "quality" of sociohistorical accuracy and analysis in order to gain "accessibility" of product for a largely white market (Rael 123–24; Smith 30). More specifically, critics faulted the film on several grounds: It misrepresents the FBI and its role in the investigation of the crimes; its narrative viewpoint excludes black main characters; and, perhaps most serious, the film deflects the essential racial nature of the events by depicting them instead as conflict between different kinds of white characters. Critics found shifting the narrative thrust from black to white characters especially ironic and troubling in light of the film's subject.

Parker's film centers on the nature of the FBI's investigative team, generating dramatic conflict from the contrast between an old-school veteran (Gene Hackman's Anderson) and a younger man who is a Kennedy liberal (Willem Defoe's Ward). Gavin Smith asserts that "using the FBI as the point of view in this story is like making the CIA the heroes of a Vietnam film about an investigation into war atrocities" (30). The resulting resolution of the narrative conflict is a logical conclusion to the film's fictional, rather than actual, conflict structure. Patrick Rael suggests that the film's focus on white heroes to the detriment of black main characters is an attribute of the freedom struggle film, which tends toward "white-obsessed stories that . . . center on the political education of white protagonists to a hitherto unknown racial reality" (120). This approach in *Mississippi Burning* perpetuates a deeper fault line, since the film ends up distorting its depiction of what the salient social conflict really was. As Gavin Smith puts it, "The irony of the film is not so much that it posits the FBI as the heroes in the crusade against segregation but that, through its central character relationship, it suggests that the real conflict going on in society in the early Sixties was between white liberals and conservatives" (30). Rael argues that a further implication of this kind of tailoring of story to fit perceived market pressures is that the resulting work distances its audience "from the very events" and people it purports to make accessible (128). The exclusion of any detailed development of black characters also limits the dimensionality of those black characters who are portrayed (120; also French 132).

Mississippi Burning's contrary realization of event and character results in alienation from, rather than proximity to, its subject. The film raises ethical concerns by reversing priorities in the most basic, known dimensions of the actual history and replacing them with strategies of plot and character that target a predominantly white audience.

The People Vs. Larry Flynt

If *JFK* and *Mississippi Burning* were faulted by critics for sins of creative addition and contradiction, then *Flynt* provides evidence of a third kind of ethical shortcoming, that is, distancing from its subject through omission. Critical concerns in this case focused on the film's efforts to depict Larry Flynt as a heroic advocate of First Amendment rights. Two basic objections emerge in the critical response to the film: In general, it valorizes hate speech, and specifically, the film waters down its depiction of the material presented in *Hustler* so that we are not given a complete picture of what Flynt's publication truly stands for.

Gloria Steinem launched the strongest attack against the film's presentation of Flynt and his primary publication; others (Miles 419; Denby, "Porn Again" 146) reiterated Steinem's objections that Forman's film whitewashed the true content of *Hustler*. In this view, the magazine is not just presenting unidealized images of nude bodies but, far worse, is urging the destruction of women through images of violence. As Steinem writes:

In this film, produced by Oliver Stone and directed by Milos Forman, *Hustler* is depicted as tacky at worst, and maybe even honest for showing full nudity. What's left out are the magazine's images of women being beaten, tortured and raped, women subject to degradations from bestiality to sexual slavery. (A 17)

Steinem argues, for example, that a 1983 *Hustler* photo essay showing a woman being gang-raped on a pool table encouraged the imitation of that crime shortly afterward in Massachusetts.

Others took further Steinem's objections to the film's selective presentation of *Hustler*'s content. The effort to show Flynt as a hero creates a setback to reopening debate about what constitutes protected speech. The thrust of this argument is that communication that advocates hate erodes, rather than contributes to, a free society, in general, and the free expression of ideas, in particular. Writers as different as Norman Podhoretz and David Denby used *Flynt* to address the issue of the quality of ideas that should be deserving of constitutional protection. Denby, for example, concludes his review of the film by noting that "the culture Larry Flynt allegedly saved should look at him as more a destroyer than a hero" because pornography, hate speech, and other forms of cultural "crud" act on our culture annihilistically, rather than constructively ("Porn Again" 150). The film omits this in its efforts to depict Flynt as a martyr. Podhoretz adds to this position the argument that the traditional metaphor of the "marketplace of ideas" might be replaced by a comparison to environmental pollution. A limit on poisons polluting the marketplace of ideas would allow a healthier cultural environment (33–34). This criticism of film suggests that the film's omissions retard, rather than advance, our understanding of free speech issues.

Kinds of Proximities

The cases of *JFK, Mississippi Burning,* and *Flynt* each show how factors affecting a docudrama's proximity to its subject create ethical repercussions. The very term *proximity* raises the question, Proximity to what? Simply to consider proximity as the extent to which a work has a factual basis does not go far enough to detail grounds on which that basis can exist. I suggest that proximity in docudrama arising from the shaping of actuality has ethical implications as it pertains to the following:

Proximity in time. Patrick Rael suggests that part of the problem with freedom struggle films is that they focus on events distant enough in the past that further kinds of alienation become easier to perpetuate.

Pictorial proximity. How strong is the modeling warrant? Casting and location selection can have as much of an impact on how a docudrama models its subject as staging of action and events.

Temporal order; plot. Selection of events and chronological structure are integral to the shaping of actual material as a classic Hollywood narrative work.

Proximity to preexisting texts. Docudramas offer explicit indications of sources;[6] the next chapter will discuss how claims of ties to prior sources can be more implicit, recurring, for example, in images of media coverage that become part of the events the work re-creates.

Proximity to living sources. The use of preexisting records raises one set of issues. The possibility of eliciting the collaboration of real-life principals and the forms that collaboration can take raise another.

Proximity to public knowledge. Works like *JFK* and *Mississippi Burning* are addressing well-known events and align themselves with the preexisting value people and events have received by their presence in contemporary culture.

This chapter opened by noting David Edgar's observation that a work's credibility depends upon its basis in fact. A consideration of the ethical issues docudramas raise suggests one further implication of the proximity of a work to its sources. The "lesson" of *Mississippi Burning* in part is that changes to augment a work's "accessibility" don't necessarily render its persuasion more effective. From the standpoint of ethics, it is equally possible that the opposite is true, that narrativity increases with a work's proximity to its sources. Edgar suggests part of what we want from a docudrama is to know how something happened. Our acceptance of the fictionalization of the real depends upon how clearly we understand and accept its degree of proximity to the known. The closer a work's proximity is to its referents, the greater will be its effectiveness as discourse, as persuasive argument.

5 | Rootable, Relatable, Promotable Docudrama: The MOW Mantra as Rhetorical Practice

Theatrically distributed feature films were the original focus of this book. It soon became clear that the sheer preponderance of movies-of-the-week "ripped from today's headlines" was impossible to ignore, and that the very factors that make docudrama rhetorically potent—the elements of docudrama form considered here so far—become even more compelling in the context of commercial television. As they fuse documentary and narrative modes, film and television docudrama have become attractive, significant means of representing both past and current actualities. That same fusion makes docudrama particularly well suited to launch persuasive argument, when its narrative structure warrants the claims developing from documentary "data." The issues of historical validity and ethical commitment entailed in the proximity of a work to the actuality it references become particularly relevant to MOW docudramas, since these works depend upon being recognized by their audience as topical and current.

This inquiry into MOW docudrama begins, accordingly, by asking why these works have been important, particularly in broadcast and cable programming from the late 1980s through the mid-to-late-1990s. When I asked that question to network executives, producers, and writers, it led to responses so similar it was comparable to listening to the reciting of a mantra: Docudrama offers effective television programming material because it is "rootable," "relatable," and "promotable." These criteria make it logical to explore further the notion of "relatability" by examining how texts use relatability as a basis for rhetorical strategies. A survey of texts shows that MOW docudrama adapts the basic character, conflict, and closure elements of classic Hollywood narrative form as configurations based on victims, the trials they undergo, and the moral articulations that arise from their experiences. Two case studies will detail how relatability strategies function in particular works. *Victim of Love: The Shannon Mohr Story* (1993) illustrates how "victim logic" establishes and develops persuasive argument about moral issues involving parental (and societal) responsibilities. *The Positively True Adventures of the Alleged Texas Cheerleader-Murdering Mom* (1993) suggests that MOW docudrama entails persuasive discourse not only about the moral implications of its immediate subject matter but also about its own nature as dramatized document.

The MOW Mantra

Since the 1980s, cable outlets steadily have taken audiences away from the three original broadcast networks. Concurrent with audience crossover, MOW docudrama has become a significant part of network and cable programming. While long form television docudrama production may have peaked in the early 1990s, it still provides a substantial portion of program material.

The production of docudrama movies, particularly by ABC, CBS, and NBC, has been a response to the loss of network audience to cable. What television executives, producers, and writers term the "rootable," "relatable," and "promotable" qualities of docudrama properties have made docudrama production an important, logical strategy for attracting audience and, for the networks, recapturing lost demographics. Due to its "rootable" material—the current and often notorious nature of its actual subject matter—docudrama can be convenient to promote. The desire for "relatable" material has led to narrower choices of subject matter. The preference for stories "based on" or "inspired by" actual events with female central characters reflects directly the ongoing effort by both network and cable to win, recapture, and maintain what they define as the core of their target audience, women between the ages of 18 and 49. The desire for rootable, promotable, relatable material also has resulted in new means of commodifying sources of story product, has fostered a "headline" concept (comparable to "high concept") approach to production and promotion, and has increased the importance of the writer as an intermediary between story subject and producer. The decrease of "torn from the headlines," "true crime" MOW production beginning in the mid-1990s, however, suggests a saturation of the market, the need for alternative strategies, and further shifts in the types of docudrama produced.

The Presence of Docudrama; Shifts in Audience

What started in the 1970s with *Brian's Song* and longer form programming such as *Roots* resulted in "true story" material by the late-1980s becoming a major staple of television film fare (Gomery 203–7). Charles Freericks, vice president of Movies and Miniseries, NBC, estimated that in 1987, docudrama amounted to 75 percent of both his and other networks' production of made-for-television movies. That amount remained around 50 percent through the early 1990s.[1]

It was also during the early- and mid-1980s that cable outlets began to attract the audience for network broadcasting (Carter D1). The erosion of the network audience has continued steadily since then (Mifflin C13). The dependence on sweeps periods has only intensified the competition for viewers between cable outlets and the original networks. During the February 1997 sweeps, for example, Fox made its strongest showing, historically, earning second place in the number of adult viewers between the ages of 18 and 49. Fox was the only network of the Big Four to increase its total number of viewers during this period (Rice 5). This performance added substantially to the pressure the major networks were already under to regain viewers. According to Victoria Sterling, a story editor and former development executive for NBC and CBS, the sweeps only fuel network efforts to get programming material on the air quickly.

Since the late-1980s, docudrama MOWs have been a logical form of programming for the networks to turn to in an effort to compete more effectively for audience. TV movies based on actual subjects are potent weapons in the ratings battles for three reasons. First, docudramas can exploit story subjects that are highly recognizable for their audience. Second, docudramas offer easy and efficient promotion possibilities. Third, docudramas have come to target directly the very audience the networks are attempting to win back.

Rootability

"Rootability" in the MOW mantra means simply that story subject matter has emerged from current events. A story's origins and possible recognizability as "news" confirms its reality status. The unlikely gains plausibility. When a life story becomes entertainment, no matter how bizarre or unlikely the events it will tell about may be, it is a "true" story, rooted in real, established occurrences.[2]

The "roots" of docudrama plots run to varying depths, depending upon how close they are to actual events, actions, and people. To codify the issue of proximity, the industry recognizes two basic categories of material: docudramas "based on" their referents and those "inspired by" actual people and occurrences. Stories "based on" true events have the closer proximity to their subjects and are governed by stricter legal guidelines than stories that are "inspired by" their sources. Generally, it will cost producers more to develop a property that is "based on" true events not only for the life rights they acquire from the principals but also to adhere to the criteria enforced by network broadcast standards departments. "Based on" scripts require extensive annotation documenting line-by-line dialogue, and character and scene descriptions.[3] "Inspired by" properties offer the attractions of lower cost and greater freedom for artistic interpretation of the original events.

The need for rootability has spawned a subindustry, dedicated to databasing potentially exploitable news stories and so linking the worlds of journalism and entertainment. The purpose of this service business is to ensure that networks and producers have quick access to likely material, including true stories not only for movies but also for news magazine shows or talk shows. A major provider of this kind of database subscription service has been Industry R&D (research and development) founded in the early-1990s by Tom Colbert. Over a period of five years, Colbert created a network of 550 newspaper and television reporters to feed stories to the IRD database. IRD categorizes and cross-references the stories it brokers by topic.

Dave Caldwell, former IRD story coordinator, explains why the service has been so effective:

> IRD has been able to find and develop over 4,000 stories in five years. [T]hey've had 30 stories optioned for movies, 15 of which have been made. That's remarkable in five years . . . to have that many stories made into movies. Because of that the industry has recognized that IRD is a valuable resource. They've got one exclusive deal with NBC for movies. If [they] found a story that was of movie caliber [they] would contact NBC immediately. [NBC] would have 24 hours.

The desire for rootable story properties then not only has resulted in the further commodification of recycled news but also has helped codify the classifications of story material. These classifications then become creative constraints that affect the choice and development of possible projects.

Promotability

The very currency of docudrama story properties also ensures their promotability, since news media have already placed these people and events on the public agenda. Thanks to news exposure, audiences probably will "know" something about the figure(s) in a story. Media promotion has only to sell the rest of the equation, that is, the promise that now we'll find out what "really happened."

Docudramas, like other MOWs, must be promoted differently from series programs. A dramatic series with a continuing story line faces promotion constraints that do not limit docudramas. Series can be promoted only during limited periods. The promotion campaign requires extensive advance planning. Multiple episodes are necessary in order to determine if there is an audience for the offering.

A television movie, on the other hand, may only have one crack at an audience but offers the flexibility of appearing whenever the schedule might accommodate it. The recognizability of docudrama subjects has allowed them to fit well within the demands of television scheduling. Comparable to "high concept" feature film marketing, these stories come preequipped with headline concepts that foreground encapsulated explanations of their subject matter. Victoria Sterling confirms that:

> Docudramas are a lot easier for networks to sell a movie audience. Their notoriety is one source of how we perceive them. TV movies . . . can be promoted based on what time of year they're airing. During sweeps they're going to be promoted much more. Out of sweeps, it could just be a week prior. You have to be able to get the promos on the air, get the TV guide out, get all your press materials out, and have people very quickly grasp what they'll be watching. They want to get them as quickly as they can, and to get them in numbers. Docudramas have really proliferated because they fit this very well.

Promotability, like rootability, has also shaped the very nature of the docudrama form. Sterling adds that "as a result of [promotion], I think there's been a retreat from trying things that are going to be riskier, more character-driven, anything that would require more difficulty on the part of the audience."

Relatability; Narrowing of the Typology

"Relatability" of a story property in the docudrama MOW mantra means that a viewer perceives a character to be "just like me" in circumstances "that could happen to me."[4] One effect of this has been, as Victoria Sterling's observation suggests, that over the last decade, the search for "relatable" properties progressively has limited the range of docudrama story types. Another, less observable, implication of "relatability" has been that the role of the scriptwriter has acquired the additional weight of acting as liaison and even as advocate for story principals.

Relatability will be a function of how a network tries to target what it perceives as its strength in addressing the basic television audience of women between the ages of 18 and 49. Sterling describes how efforts to link audience and story operated in her work in network story departments:

> The networks always hope for a core of relatability to the main characters in a movie. This was primarily more laid out at CBS when I was there than at ABC, when I was there. At ABC we had a lot more diversity in the movies because it was a different kind of audience. They also were oriented more to family. They would cast movies with both male and female leads. This allowed them to have movies centered more on family stories. Stories at that time would fill family objectives. There was always woman in jeopardy, family in jeopardy, child in jeopardy. You had your basic thriller, your character piece, and your prestige piece. At that time [late-1980s] the leads were also much older: Joanna Kern, Jaclyn Smith, Tyne Daly—the women in those roles were in their 30s, if not close to 40.
>
> They were programming primarily for women, for mothers, housewives, women not working outside the home, and most of the dramas had a domestic orientation. The stories were primarily domestic settings. Things that would take place in a suburban community. Suburban Chicago, Atlanta, Detroit.

A corollary of the suburban setting has been to cast characters as white and middle-class, regardless of their actual race and social status, as a way of maximizing property "relatability."

The narrowing of story types in part has been a result of changes in network management. In 1994–1995, CBS attempted to recuperate audience it was losing to NBC by redefining its niche of the target audience. Sterling notes that in the early-1990s, the CBS audience included rural and older viewers. With a drastic turnover in management in 1994, CBS attempted unsuccessfully to mimic its competition:

> There was a big mandate because they were starting to lose audience, and NBC was competing very strongly. In a very rash and brash move [CBS execs] decided they were going to go all young. Go for a young audience. In order to go young they decided they were going to utilize younger actors, mimicking what NBC was doing. NBC started it, and they started beating out CBS for the movie ratings.

The shift to stories targeting younger, rather than older, audience (and requiring a commensurate shift from casting older to younger actors) has also been accompanied by a stricter focus on female-centered stories. Through the mid- and late-1980s, docudrama stories were more diverse and inclusive. Dennis Nemec, whose docudrama screenwriting credits begin in the early-1980s, has seen this change in relation to his own work:

> TV docudramas have become . . . female oriented. If you look at [my] other docudramas, in *A Long Way Home* (1981), a family is broken up and tries to get itself together, but it's a boy's story about how he can find his brother and sister. *Murder in Coweta County* (1983) was a crime drama, your basic good guy, black hat vs. white hat, and a period piece. *The Ray Mancini Story* (1985) was a boxer story. *A Case of Deadly Force* (1986) was an attorney story. *Held Hostage* was a political story in some ways, but with a female lead. The whole demographics of it, in my experience of it, began to shift toward the female lead.

In light of the mission to produce a "relatable" product, the scriptwriter's role assumes the functions of an intermediary. The writer represents the interests of the story principals in the production process, as well as in the completed script. The added responsibility potentially makes the docudrama screenwriter increasingly vulnerable to ethical dilemmas. Authenticity of the script necessarily begins with the writer-subject relationship. "Authenticity" cuts both ways for the writer, who is faced with, on the one hand, the need to present the substance of the real-life principal and, on the other hand, the need to shape creatively a believable, "relatable" character in a fiction narrative.

Typically, in a docudrama project, it is the producer who initiates the production process by negotiating with the principal or principals for their life rights. The producer then enters into reporting relationships with the network development executive and, indirectly, the network vice president, who ultimately green-lights the production, all based upon a satisfactory script.[5] It falls upon the writer to work most directly and extensively with the real-life principals of the story not only in gathering the material that will become the script but also in explaining to that person what happens to the stuff of their life once it becomes part of a film.

Writer Bruce Miller (*The Stranger Beside Me*, ABC, 1995) believes it is necessary to exclude the real-life principals from the scriptwriting process once he has finished his research with them. He describes the closeness he reaches with his subjects during the research phase as "gut-wrenching"; however, as he begins to shape a script, he tells his principals that "they are dealing with other priorities than the truth" in the need to present a dramatically effective, engaging story.

While this approach relieves the pressure of responding to the concerns of story sources, it limits the potential of their further collaboration, as well as leaving them susceptible to exploitation. Writer Tom Cook

(*Tuskegee Airmen,* HBO, 1995; *Forgotten Evil,* ABC, 1996) argues that the ties he develops in working with real-life principals becomes the basis for protecting their interests:

> One of the things that really drives us crazy, that really hurts us emotionally, is that we develop relationships with the sources. We're the ones that go out and spend days and weeks in the homes of the people who have been killed or lost a child, or [have] had something awful happen to them, and we develop the friendships with those people, friendships that are sometimes not respected by the director and the producers that come after us. I have been in a story meeting with the producer or the network people, for whom admittedly this is just one of a dozen things they're dealing with, and they say, well, why can't we have this guy die a little earlier? And I'm thinking back to the real people: I sat in their living room and wept over this event that happened. We'd be holding hands and crying over this horrible event. Now the network people, for their reasons which make sense to them, want to change this and move it around and manipulate it. What am I going to go back and tell the sources? That this is what's going to happen to their story? Sometimes I can protect them. Sometimes I just won't do it. But I've had the experience where people will look and me and say, "That never happened. We never told you that." And I have to try to explain to them what *our* needs are, what the network's needs are, and that's very difficult.

Dennis Nemec believes that part of his work is to prepare his story subjects for the transformations their material must undergo when he scripts it:

> I have found, without exception, that if you explain to people why you're doing what you're doing, they understand it. If you treat them like they're idiots, like, hey you don't know about the TV business, so I don't want to be bothered by you, then you've cut them off. You've lost both their trust and their unsullied input. I once had a producer say, "Let them see it when it comes out." I find if you tell them why you are making certain changes, they understand it. Little by little, scene by scene—you prepare them for what's coming. They understand. If I say, "Look, the network wants this to happen. We know that you know the guy was a bad guy from day one. But that doesn't give the network the suspense it needs. So we're going to play it that you weren't quite sure." They understand. And as long as they see that you're on their side, they'll continue to be supportive, which helps me, because I need them for those kind of specific details which only they can provide. Those wonderful details really give the piece an authenticity that may take the place of some of the accuracy that's missing, so that it has a tonal authenticity, even if detail and fact may have been bent to accommodate ninety-five pages.

So I feel good about that in terms of my moral compass, but I let them know what's going to happen.

Tristine Rainer, a docudrama producer/writer, who has also published *Your Life as Story* (1997), agrees that it is the scriptwriter's responsibility not only to enlist the collaboration of the subject if the script is to be authentic but also, and even more so, to foreground the essential uniqueness of that person's story:

> I feel everybody has a completely unique life story. In fact, I hold this idea of story, of personal mythology, as something sacred. Each person has a main core story, and that is their contribution. To me, it is a profound concept. My principal allegiance and bond in working with someone's true story is to that individual's emotional truth.

The practical constraints the docudrama scriptwriter faces in creating "relatable" characters and plot structure then lead logically to ethical considerations. The writer must balance the need to respect the "truth" of a principal's life story with the need to shape a dramatically compelling character. Ultimately, the value of the story as history will stem not only from its proximity to actuality but also from the extent to which an audience will find what it has to say about that actuality at all compelling.

Further Shifts—Current/Future Trends

Docudrama movies-of-the-week have been a central strategy in the efforts by networks and cable outlets to capture and maintain television audience. The same economic constraints that have led to the production of rootable, relatable, promotable TV movies through the mid-1990s also determine the subsequent direction of docudrama. This is evident in the decreasing amount of docudrama currently on the air, and the concurrent shift in story types from "true crime" to more character-driven, more "inspired by," and more fully fictionalized pieces.

Through 1995 and 1996, approximately 11 percent of all movies available on broadcast and cable television fit into some form of docudrama.[6] Charles Freericks estimated that in 1998, while CBS probably would base one-fourth of its movie production on true stories, NBC had dropped from 40 percent in 1995 to 10 to 15 percent in 1997, and reduced 1998 docudrama MOW production to 10 percent of its output. ABC "is somewhere in between, but also dropping fast." The reductions were due to the market reaching its saturation point in 1995.

A number of writers and producers believe that the "true story" market has changed to support less crime-oriented, more inspirational stories.

The turn away from "true crime," "ripped from the headlines" story types is due to increasing scrutiny of network and cable outlets through the rating system initiated in early 1997, and continuing pressure from special interest groups to tone down violent programming. In this view, the market favors looser, more fictionalized stories because of the lower cost (fewer rights to acquire) and less rigorous legal demands of "inspired by true event" material. Whether such a modified strategy gratifies the needs of TV program providers to win elusive demographics, or the needs of the audience to be told compelling explanations of events and phenomena of their daily lives, or both, remains to be seen.

The Rhetoric of Relatability in MOW Docudrama

Movie-of-the-week docudramas encompass a wide range of diverse topics, situating stories based on actual people and events often within established narrative frameworks (disaster, biography, courtroom drama, history, etc.)[7] In order to map out the common ground this work occupies, as well as to relate it to feature films, my analysis approaches MOW docudrama as a recognizable narrative mode characterized by its rhetorical functions. To do so is justified, particularly because docudrama producers conceive of their work explicitly as a process of constructing persuasive arguments. In theorizing their projects as "rootable," "promotable," and "relatable" stories, the creators and packagers of docudrama telefeatures are developing persuasive appeals comparable to those in theatrically distributed docudramas: Stories based on actuality (data) qualify as rootable and promotable, appealing to their audience through relatability strategies (warrants) that frame the arguments (claims) the works ultimately advocate.

Given the medium they are created for, MOW docudramas tend to tell "personal" stories. Docudrama MOWs are, of course, offering us some actual person's "true story"; however, made-for-television films in general tend to operate on a "human" scale. For example, Gary Edgerton notes that "[t]he individualized and informal depiction of everyday characters in an assortment of medium shots and close-ups quickly became the forte of the TV movie, more so than in any other feature film form" (118). Douglas Gomery concurs and points out (in his analysis of *Brian's Song* as a prototypical MOW docudrama) that the form works "by reducing [early-1970s racial] issue[s] to the most personal level" (213). Todd Gitlin suggests that MOWs tell "personal stories an audience will take as revelations of the contemporary" (164). Social and historical issues may emerge implicitly but remain secondary to the work of using narrative form to thrust a story's real-life principals into the bright public light of prime time television. The traditional feature film biopic, by comparison, has tended to consider well-known, "great" subjects within the cultural, social, and historical contexts informing their stories.[8] The "personal" approach of a MOW docudrama, on the other hand, argues why we should understand that the material of the life of someone otherwise "just like us" has become exemplary. The prominence of people's names in the titles of so many MOW docudramas indicates the same kind of effort to interrelate character and historical context as the traditional biopic. Marcia Landy suggests that "the exploration of the proper name as signature is relevant to an examination of biography as a means of facilitating a critical interrogation of the social forces that get erased through the valorization of individual agency as a major determinant of history" (152). Leger Grindon further links this view of history to the material circumstances of production:

> Such economic factors as the star system promoted this concept [of valorizing individual characters as causal agents in biopics]. So did the analytical editing style, in which the force of performance and modes of personal interaction (e.g., the shot-countershot, point-of-view formats, and responsive close-ups) serve to narrow the focus from the expansive mise-en-scene of the spectacle to the nuances of character. (23)

The very fact of the production of MOW docudrama raises other basic questions about audience and the value it places on "personal" stories. Why will an audience listen to the story at all? In light of the work's persuasive strategies, what is the story it tells attempting to persuade its audience of?

MOW docudramas share common persuasive strategies in offering us contemporary moral cautionary tales. One purpose here will be to show how, in creating the underlying "relatability" of a story, the mode of MOW docudrama adapts character, conflict, and closure, three of the defining elements of classic Hollywood film narrative form, to function as persuasive strategies. In light of the large number of MOW docudramas produced by network and cable outlets, I have limited my survey to a representative sample distributed as the Lifetime Network's January 1996 "Real Story Weekend." The Lifetime selections include works from both major network and cable producers and illustrate a variety of docudrama narrative subtypes (disaster, disease, abuse, crime, etc.)[9] that show MOW persuasive strategies at work. As a means to accomplish persuasive ends, MOW docudrama's rhetorical strategies evident across various kinds of stories include exemplification (we are told, in essence, a story of survival—characters have endured an experience that renders the telling of their story necessary and justifiable); articulation (a survival narrative culminates in a moment of summation—a literal or figurative trial creates a forum for stating the moral issues that arise from the survival story); and, ultimately, clarification (narrative closure suggests that a moral perspective has been resolved in the world the audience shares with the story subjects).

Relatability and Narrative

Since the industry conceptualizes MOW docudrama product as rootable, relatable, and promotable, it is not surprising that it places these values at the center of what writer/producer Cynthia Cherbak calls the "core concept" that drives the creation of a specific work.[10] Each element of the industry pragmatic emphasizes how extensively MOW docudramas are conceived as rhetorical works.

The MOW docudrama writers that I interviewed universally labeled their works as "women in jeopardy" and "she was just like us until . . ." kinds of stories. Writing as early as 1983, Todd Gitlin refers offhandedly to how MOW docudramas, the "woman in jeopardy genre," tell "morality tale[s]" (168). By depicting predominantly female characters in some form of jeopardy, MOW docudrama's "relatable" material depends upon a combination of warrants to forward its arguments. The promotable linkage of the story to known, reported events that have entered the public agenda provides one kind of warrant. Presenting people in a state of jeopardy provides another. The very logic of the response to the threat posed when one is in jeopardy (escape; elimination of threat) warrants further argument, positioning viewers to find in their very difference from the story being told some form of instruction through moral clarification. Steve Sohmer, who has worked as a writer, producer, and network executive, addresses the rhetorical function of employing jeopardy as a narrative premise:

> The archetypal promo does not dwell on the pain and suffering of being raped, abandoned, or having your children taken away. The archetypal promo says, "When she was x" (violated, robbed, whatever, three seconds of that), "she fought back" (and then you get twenty-seven seconds of that). It's the way the woman fights back against these things.

For writer Tom Cook, the rhetorical thrust of the MOW docudrama is to provide instruction through example:

> But there are still even today stories about people whose emotional problems are driven by ordinary events, who come across a situation where they can't

cope, and TV movies do a good job of instructing people about how to deal with difficulty in their lives, and how bad luck and ill fortune impact people, even if it's not their fault, and how they can cope courageously and fight back. TV, with all of its faults, has an enormous cathartic and empathetic value for a lot of people in this country. In terms of domestic issues, everyday issues— what do I do if my son's kidnapped—this is how people learn how to behave, how they distinguish between good behavior and bad behavior. It has enormous cathartic value.[11]

Before exploring how specific MOW docudramas attempt to appeal to their target audiences through relatability strategies, it will be helpful to define "relatability" in more theoretical terms, and to trace the sources of "relatability" to more traditional literary and rhetorical "identification" theories. Both types of identification theory emphasize the formal parameters of a text that allow a reader to feel connected to it. These theories, when applied to film, presume a Lacanian kind of viewer-image relationship in which the roots of readership begin with identification, the internalizing of perceived similarities and differences of self and other.[12] From this implicit premise, identification theories strive to explain how the recognition of interrelation of self and other functions.[13] Norman N. Holland, for example, in *The Dynamics of Literary Response,* views identification as a creative investment a reader makes in response to tensions (needs and desires) perceived as held in common with a character:

> The more clearly a given character embodies my tensions, the more the work of art stimulates those tensions in me; the more I have those tensions in myself anyway—why, then, the more real a given character will seem. He will, ultimately seem as real to me as I myself, for out of my own drives and needs for defense, I have created him. (274–75)

The power of identification stems from a dynamic of projection and reception in reading a character:

> Thus, our so-called "identification" with a literary character is actually a complicated mixture of projection and introjection, and of taking in from the character certain drives and defenses that are really objectively "out there" and of putting into him feelings that are really our own, "in here." (278–79)

Identification becomes an element of persuasive argument when this investment in character established through perceived similarities of a sender and receiver encourages acceptance of a message, creating a persuasive effect. Kenneth Burke, for example, views rhetoric itself as communication that produces "change in attitude or action through identification" (Foss 158). In Burke's view, identification arises from shared ideas and experiences, the very "substance" of what gives us our identities.[14] Identification occurs with another when we see our interests as joined. Even when we identify with someone, however, we retain a sense of our individuality. We can become "substantially one" with another while remaining unique entities (Burke 21). As we watch characters on screen, their actions will be persuasive to the extent that we perceive that we have important common ground.

Relatability strategies in MOW docudrama borrow elements from both literary and rhetorical thinking. Giving a viewer a means to "relate" to a character in a docudramatic re-creation draws on sufficient commonality between viewer and character that the film's claim, its purpose for presenting this personal story, will be accessible. "Commonality" stems from middle-roading characterization (tending to depict white, middle-class, mostly female characters living in suburban settings) regardless of the demographics of the real-life principals. Tom Cook, among those writers who describe the "archetypal" TV movie as the "she was just like us until . . ." movie, adds that "'Us' is upper-middle-class white women, living in the suburbs of the cities." Several producers and writers noted that for characters to be promotable, they must appear to be "real average people." The persuasive project of the MOW docudrama will be to argue, through the relatability of the example set by the personal story unfolding before us, which of the available options for thought, feeling, and behavior ought to be most desirable. In the traditional spirit of melodrama, the resolution of the "character in jeopardy" narrative will give the purpose of the story a moral resolution; "relating" to a character—comparing ourselves to them, placing ourselves in their position for the duration of the narrative—clarifies and reinforces notions of what people "like us" ought to do when confronted with dilemmas of choice and action. Relatability strategies will warrant the work's persuasive appeal through reference (the link of the story to the known, actual event framework that allows promotion of the product) and definition (placing character and action in moral contexts).

The ways "relatability" provides the conceptual core for docudrama's positioning of its viewer will be evident by examining how relatability strategies function in narrative practice. As "personal" stories, MOW docudramas fit comfortably within the conventional narrative framework circumscribed by the mode of classic Hollywood cinema. In *The Classical Hollywood Cinema: Film Style and Mode of Production to 1960*, David Bordwell, Janet Staiger, and Kristin Thompson show how classic

Hollywood narrative films exhibit consistent features stemming from the overall consistency of telling character-driven stories. These include the portrayal of character motivation through conventions of psychological realism, an emphasis on character desire as a causal force in the development of the story, and the working of narrative development toward some degree of closure. The analysis that follows of *Shannon Mohr* will show how docudrama narrative uses relatability strategies, placing those "events of the narrative in their presumed spatial, temporal and causal relationships" in order to direct "the hypothesis-constructing activity of the viewer's reading of the narrative" toward the claims the film advocates (Bordwell, Staiger, and Thompson 12). Docudrama, as a mode of presentation,[15] manifests the basic defining characteristics of the classic Hollywood narrative film (centrality of character desire and psychological realism; plot development through chains of clear chronology and causality; privileging of narrative closure).[16] It is narrative, however, with persuasive purpose.

Character Strategies: The Survivor Role as Exemplification

The Lifetime sample suggests that there are several necessary qualifications of the industry typing of MOW docudramas as telling stories of "victims" who "fight back." Victims, whether of disease, accident, or circumstance, experience harmful consequences of conditions usually beyond their control. Half of the central characters (those whose stories are being told) in the Lifetime sample qualify as victims of external circumstances.[17] Shannon Mohr, for example, is seduced and murdered by Dave, the deceitful suitor who marries her only for insurance benefits; Truddi Chase, in *Voices Within: The Lives of Truddi Chase,* has adopted multiple personalities to cope with the psychological and sexual abuse she experienced as a child. Dawn Smith, in *A Nightmare in Columbia County,* is stalked by her sister's murderer. The dozens of passengers of the "miracle flight" are bashed and battered by their aircraft's disintegrating fuselage and jet stream before the crippled plane can land.

The role becomes more complex in the other half of the sample because the central characters become noteworthy—become story subjects—not as victims at all but as perpetrators. Their actions may create immediate victims; however, these attain the status only of minor characters (clearly these are not *their* stories). What is important is that to varying degrees, these perpetrators victimize themselves. Consider the following:

In *Stay the Night,* Mike Kettman, a high school student, murders the husband of Jimmie Sue Finger, an older woman (the mother of a girl he is dating), who becomes his lover. He is sentenced to life in jail.[18] Amy Fisher similarly shoots (but in this case only wounds) her rival, Mary Jo Buttafuoco, the wife of Amy's older intended, Joey. Mary Jo is partially paralyzed. Amy is convicted of first-degree assault and sentenced to a five- to ten-year imprisonment. Wanda Holloway, the alleged Texas cheerleader-murdering mom, enters negotiations through her ex-brother-in-law to hire a hit man to kill Amber Heath, her daughter's rival, and Amber's mother, Verna. While the intended victims remain untouched and continue to pursue Amber's career as a high school cheerleader, Wanda is tried and found guilty (but her conviction is overturned).

The self-victimizers all lead emphatically comfortable, middle-class lives. If anything, they are overprotected by parents or spouses.[19] Uncontrollable outside forces do not intervene to disrupt the normalcy of their lives. Their stories offer explorations of fallibility. We learn how, why, and to what extent any of us (and/or our children) are susceptible to desires difficult to resist.

Whether victims of external or internal circumstances, the central characters in the Lifetime sample ultimately become exemplary not because they are victims but because they are survivors. The meaning and value of "survival" vary with specific narrative purpose. Survival may be literally the key issue (for the survivors of the miracle landing, for example, or for Truddi Chase, who is not simply an incest survivor but reclaims her life after she outgrows her desire to wreak revenge on her abusive stepfather). Their obligations as survivors drive parents to find justice for their children (the parents of Shannon Mohr strive to find and help convict her murderer; Blanche Kettman, Mike's mother, must make Mike see that Jimmie Sue does not love him before he will help expose her complicity in her husband's murder). Amy Fisher and Wanda Holloway may have only attempted (or considered attempting) murder, directing the thrust of their stories toward the basic questions that arise about the quality of their lives in the aftermath of their own actions.

In all cases, relatability may begin with central characters in some way(s) appearing to be "just like us"; however, it is their status as survivors that argues to us to attend to their stories. Argument by example is only the initial strategy in the process of convincing us that the story we are watching offers something exemplary, something that we can learn from. The appeal of the story inheres partly in the opportunity it affords to see what survival on these terms necessitates, warranted by the "true story" premise (this "really happened"). By witnessing the ordeals that characters are put through or put themselves through, we are prepared for the articulation the trial process will present.

Strategies of Plot Development: Trial and Articulation

The ordeals that will constitute the figurative or literal trials in these works are developed through three interrelated formal strategies: development of viewpoint structures, particularly through flashbacks; display of character activity (showing characters' responses to circumstances that "test" them);[20] and, finally, a "trial" phase through which a forum arises for articulating the meaning of past and present actions the story has shown. The "character in jeopardy" premise for selecting and shaping these narratives itself places plot development within a moral framework.

A flashback structure to develop narrative chronology predominates the Lifetime sample. Five of the eight works use flashbacks systematically.[21] As a common strategy of development, the flashback conveys multiple implications. A flashback structure allows the narrative to claim not just an "objective" but also an "inside" perspective. The ability to shift from present to past demonstrates that survival in some state has occurred; furthermore, it demonstrates that the story we are about to see will divulge the cost of survival. A basic purpose of the story will be to share the wisdom and understanding the survivor(s) may have acquired. To do so requires the kind of access to character experience a flashback makes possible by creating the opportunity to compare and contrast past and present thought and behavior. In each instance, the structure serves to underscore a different claim as to why the specific survival story is exemplary.[22]

The flashback structure contributes to the sense that the story can give us the "inside view" as to "what really happened" through its joining of past and present. The sample shows several kinds of past/present interrelations. In *Miracle Landing* and *Voices Within: The Lives of Truddi Chase*, the thrust of the comparison is to show how character responses in the present are connected directly to past causes (training experiences have given the pilot and copilot of the airliner the abilities to cope with the present emergency; the terrorization of Truddi Chase as a little girl—her stepfather stalking her in the woods, shooting her pet rabbit, and attacking her physically—explains her need for therapy in the present day). The reliability of these memories is never an issue. Working in an opposite, *Rashomon*-like way, *Beyond Control: The Amy Fisher Story* explores the certainty of memory by comparing how two characters have different recollections of the same events (Amy's and Joey's views of first meeting each other at his body shop, for example, diverge in showing the kind and degree of interest he may have in her). *Shannon Mohr* and *The Positively True Adventures of the Alleged Texas Cheerleader-Murdering Mom* (*Mohr* and *TCMM*) develop modified flashback styles by finding alternative locations for past images held within the mind of a remembering character. Shannon Mohr is dead, and her husband, Dave, a proven liar who denies everything alleged against him, is on trial for her murder. The prosecutor describes to the jury the forensic evidence that suggests Dave injected Shannon with a paralyzing drug. We view the images of their past actions the prosecutor's summary descriptions create. Through his inferential reasoning, we and the jury see how Shannon was positioned to witness her own murder. Wanda Holloway's statements during a present-day interview about her past actions are followed by scenes that depict but also surpass what she is saying, allowing the narrative to establish comparisons and contrasts the perceptions of the character would not allow (see discussion of these films below).

Flashback frames explain how and why characters can undergo the trials we see in the present. The overall process of "trying" characters entails testing them, testing their response, and then escalation of effort as their literal or figurative trials work toward culmination.[23] Characters are tested by often-proscribed desires that tempt them (Mike Kettman pursues Jimmie Sue, a married woman, from the first moment he sees her; Amy desires Joey Buttafuoco, a married man, in much the same way; Wanda wants her daughter to succeed at any cost; Shannon Mohr marries Dave after a whirlwind courtship). To fail the test of temptation means an initial transgression of morality or common sense (adulterous affairs; bending rules; precipitous marriage) leading to breaking the law (murder in one instance; considered and/or attempted murder in the others). Truddi Chase's recovered memories of abuse test and explain her sanity throughout her story and place her, at the film's climax, on the doorstep of her stepfather, ready to attain her revenge with the murderously sharp scissors in her hand.

Displays of effort convey the process of "testing" characters. In several instances, the effort belongs not to the character whose story we are ostensibly being told but to those who move into the center of the story to fulfill a role of catalyst or facilitator. After her death, Shannon Mohr's parents seemingly dedicate their lives to the pursuit and capture of Dave, who has, we find, a consistent pattern of courtship, lies, death, cashed-in insurance policies, and fugitive identities. Only when they've gathered enough evidence can they convince the prosecutor to pursue the case.

Similarly, Blanche Kettman becomes the main character in *Stay the Night* after her son has been convicted of murder. To the astonishment of her family, Blanche strives to become Jimmie Sue's best friend in order to entrap her. Blanche must sell her plan not only to her husband and daughters and to law enforcement but also (and even more difficult) to her son, who refuses to believe Jimmie Sue has turned on him, even when she flaunts a new boyfriend. The telling of Amy Fisher's story becomes the job of a reporter who becomes interested in the case and the particularly harsh legal treatment Amy receives. The very film we are seeing about Wanda Holloway testifies to the demands placed upon her to justify what she intended to do about her daughter's cheerleading rival.

Six of the eight works in the sample situate the consequences of the tests of temptation and transgression in courtroom trials; thus it is not surprising that so much of the effort we see central characters expending is investigative and/or persuasive. Trials provide a forum for articulation and judgment. The process of trial and outcome ultimately verifies the meaning of survival and explains why a case is exemplary. The trials (whether literal or figurative) in these works fulfill three interrelated functions: First, trials help connect the film's representation of events to public record, reiterating the link to actuality the docudrama claims; second, trials provide a structure for the telling of someone's story (and create a rationale and basis for a subsequent telling, the film we are seeing) thereby asserting existential authenticity through narrative; and third, a trial necessarily moves toward verdict, indicating how issues raised by the story can be resolved.

A trial that provides a story's actuality anchor contributes to the promotability of a work (an audience has already heard about the "cheerleader-murdering mom") and, consequently, its veracity.[24] Promotability argues that the place of the story on the public record prevents its account from erroneous invention. Too much is known already, and conversely, the particularity of events cannot be a fiction, no matter (or perhaps because of) how unusual or bizarre those events might be. The narrative is sufficiently dependent upon "known" material that the composite and speculative inventions it does create must be probable. *Mohr, Fisher, Nightmare,* and *TCMM* go even further, bolstering their narrative sources in public records by incorporating explicit reference to the original media accounts of these events.

As much as a trial offers a ritualistic opportunity for explanation—at last, we are to find out if, how, and why a transgression of law and/or morality occurred—only one of the works in the sample allows courtroom proceedings to provide completion to the process of righting the wrongs the work has told about. By re-creating Shannon Mohr's last moments, the prosecutor's closing arguments in the case provide her point of view, the last, most conclusive piece in the puzzle of how to understand her death. In other works, trials only tell part of the story. Mike Kettman's trial ends halfway through *Stay;* Blanche must convince both Mike and Malone, the detective who has investigated the case, not once but twice, to set up a visit to jail in which Jimmie Sue will acknowledge out loud (and on tape) to Mike her complicity in her husband's murder. The testimony in Amy Fisher's trial seems only to skim the surface of the events we see re-created in flashback; however, the most important summation of what has happened comes not in the courtroom but at the film's close, when the reporter who has followed the story confronts Amy's mother and blames her spoiling of her daughter for what has happened. Wanda Holloway's conviction and fifteen-year sentence (thrown out because of a mistrial) are only a contributing part to the perspective the overall film we are seeing provides in its combined re-creation of news coverage, interviews, talk show appearances, and private encounters between characters. The film as a whole provides comparison and reflection necessary to articulate the value and meaning of what we've seen. In a similar way, *Voices* uses an epistolary structure (we hear throughout the film Truddi's letters to "Stanley," her therapist) to present Truddi's "case" to him and to us; here the resolution occurs not in the brief confrontation between Truddi and Paul on his doorstep but rather at a Christmas party between patient and therapist that closes the film. Truddi refuses to accept the standard therapeutic plan to "integrate" the voices she hears into a more unitary identity because they are what have allowed her to cope with the exigencies that have shaped her life. Throughout the story, she calls them her "troops," because they have always come to her rescue; besides, she tells her external therapist, "we outnumber you."

The trial process necessitates, even if it doesn't include, these moments of climactic articulation that clarify and resolve the moral issues story events have raised.[25] Even *Miracle Landing* has a late moment in which a crew member straightens out an FBI agent who questions the events on the plane and the pilot and copilot's response to them. Despite the fact that this is what we've seen for over an hour, the brief speech confirms the skill and courage necessary to pull plane and passengers through.

In each case, effort from catalytic characters, facilitators who take up the causes of victim/survivors, culminates in articulation, fully framing the actions of testing, response, and trial that constitute the narrative. Articulation allows a final validation of the survival story. Docudrama narratives create moral context systematically. The "test" that confronts characters early in their stories poses the question of whether or not they will do the right thing, so that the test in effect sets up a moral trial in advance of actual litigation that may follow. The legal proceedings we see represented in *Mohr, Stay, Fisher,* and *TCMM* underline the potential fallibility of courtroom processes. The rituals of evidence and testimony are subject to patriarchal prejudice and unreliable or incomplete presentation. The culminating moments resolving these stories both verify and clarify that even if justice may have been only partial in the courtroom, it has now achieved a complete hearing. Articulation brings everything to light that may have been hidden (what Shannon Mohr saw; what Jimmie Sue said; what Mrs. Fisher needs to be told), thereby righting what went wrong at the outset.

Narrative resolution through trial and eventual articulation then asserts the final validity of the survivor story. Telling the story through the form of docudrama traces the process from victimization (and often the accompanying powerlessness of the victim) to validation. When characters such as Shannon Mohr and Shari Smith are afforded the opportunity to "speak" from beyond the grave, their eulogies are particularly moral remembrances. The narrative arc of docudrama follows the main character and others central to their story as they undergo a process of enlightenment. Articulation itself grows out of action and effort responding to someone's initial victimization. Articulation may be a component of the work's melodramatic excess, its overstatement of what the story has shown to be at stake; however, it is also a warranted outgrowth of the story's roots in actuality. In each instance, these "true story" narratives make a case for the validation of the individual whose life shows us an example of the results of confronting powerful forces exceeding individual control, the trials faced as a consequence, and the utility of subsequent response.

The articulation of wrongful deed and rightful action it necessitates is warranted by the stories' links to actuality, and its rhetorical function then is instructive. We have been shown what went wrong and how; accordingly, seven of the works in this group appeal directly to parents *(Mohr; Stay; Fisher; Voices; TCMM; Nightmare; and Desperate Rescue)* to compare their own actions, decisions, and values to those shown, and to learn from these examples. The characters in these works make moral issues both material, because they are linked to an external actuality, and accessible, because they are presented and clarified through the form of one person's story. Through our hearing of what story subjects have endured in the past and may have to continue to confront in the future, their stories not only validate them as individuals but also argue that the narration of their stories contributes to the ongoing process of threatening and restoring the balance of right and wrong in the world the films suggest we share with them.

Relatability Strategies in *Victim of Love: The Shannon Mohr Story*

> I think it's a matter of creating rootable characters that the audience is going to empathize with. It's that fighting back.
> —Steve Sohmer, personal interview, Mar. 1997

> The big audience for true stories demographically is female. That's why there are so many damsel-in-distress stories. "Keep your hands off my kid" stories.
> —Abraham Tetenbaum, personal interview, Mar. 1997

The fact that a story is being told as a MOW docudrama indicates a process of valorization and an accompanying moral system. The status implicit in the production system's selection and subsequent realization of an individual's story offers a prima facie case for the "exemplary" nature of the material ("this story is worth watching over countless others"). For someone to tell us their story allows them to say, in effect, "here is what I did." Subsequent narrative events define those actions and their consequences, allowing the possibility of comparison and contrast of what a person has "done" to what that figure, now a character in a narrative, "ought to do." The narrative interplay of desires, obstacles, and actions taken out of possible options allows docudrama characters to provide moral reference points. The trials they undergo and the verdicts reached place in perspective whatever threat may have arisen to the balance of right and wrong in the world of the film.

Victim Logic

MOW docudrama shows a marked preference for "victim" stories. The case we are about to see promises to be exemplary in the way it will illustrate the causes and effects of victimization. The task of bringing victimization to light creates a reciprocal logic, the logic of witnessing. The audience, through the means of the narrative, sees what has befallen someone "just like" us. The victim narrative positions us as spectators who become witnesses. The film places us on scene, allows us to be present at the story's key events. We "know" what occurred; we have been granted access to evidence that eventually could be brought to light. Witnessing mediates between the perpetration of wrong and the possibility of remedy. Our fortune is that we are warned because we have seen what happened. The story's warning offers itself as an opportunity for empowerment. The knowledge it affords points toward the possibility of corrective action. The story of someone's suffering argues for what it will take to validate his or her life. Through its relatability strategies, a victim story becomes exemplary in depicting powerlessness as a premise to argue for the terms of empowerment. The narrative's basic persuasive claim then is simply this: Learn from what happened here.

In *Mohr,* the reciprocal logics of victimization and witnessing warrant the work's claims about justice and familial roles. Its warrants structure narrative development through the logic of victimization and position viewers within and outside of the film as witnesses. The process of providing witness ultimately validates what survives Shannon Mohr. Characteristic of MOW docudrama, the film's persuasive appeal relies upon relatability created through the strategies of depicting survival, articulating what survival means, and claiming the restoration of moral order that articulation clarifies.[26]

Mohr asserts only in part that its antagonist, Dave Davis, should not be allowed to get away with murder. The film also argues that what can be seen and heard provides knowledge and truth when it can be presented as witness testimony. The logic of victim and witness structuring the film's narrative makes evidence visual, accessible, and allows the film to claim that the truth will emerge and justice will operate. What Dave Davis tries to hide, an investigation fueled by the desire to right his wrongs will reveal. The logic of the witness narrative shifts wrongful action from private to public knowledge. Expressing what has been witnessed literally brings the truth to light.

Mohr adds a further, specifically docudramatic, warrant to its depiction of the process of gathering, allocating, and confirming the viewpoints of witnesses. Throughout, the narrative asserts that it is not a self-enclosed fiction but a true story, rooted not only in actual events but also in actual media events. The narrative anchors itself to actuality through its reference to an external text, the *Unsolved Mysteries* television program, that not only was a catalyst in the original story but also initiated the MOW docudrama production we are watching. In order to tell fully the story of Shannon Mohr, reality TV has spawned docudrama. The actuality anchor implicates the "viewing public" of the original program as potential witnesses. It underlines claims for the truth value of what we are witnessing in the telefeature, arguing from this truth that our knowledge of "what really happened" and whatever we might learn from it—whether it be about spousal trust, parental responsibility, or the slow but ultimately inevitable operation of justice—clarifies the larger importance of Shannon Mohr's life.

Victims as Witnesses

At one point in *Mohr,* Detective Brooks comments, "Witness? Shannon Mohr's not the witness here, she's the victim." Clearly, an equally apt phrasing for the work's subtitle might be "The Survivors of Love." The Shannon Mohr story illustrates the excessive clarity with which MOW docudrama narrative links the roles of victim and survivor with witnesses acting as intermediaries. Through the film's relatability strategies, the process of providing witness allows the experiences of victimization and survival to become exemplary. The point of Shannon Mohr's story is twofold. First, the story shows that she is "survived" by her parents and by whatever statements and forensic data that testify to her victimization. This testimony provides the lessons in trust and responsibility her case illustrates. Second, the story affirms the value of the role of the media, when it becomes an aid to the process of providing testimony. Opposite from a MOW such as *The Positively True Adventures of the Alleged Texas Cheerleader-Murdering Mom,* which incorporates self-consciously the role of the media in the narration of its story in order to expose and question the influence of media on its culture, *Mohr* mounts a testament to the heroic role the media play in bringing a victim story to light.

What, essentially, is a "victim"? The primary meanings include the following:

1. A living being sacrificed to a deity or in the performance of a religious rite
2. Someone injured, destroyed, or sacrificed under any of various conditions
3. Someone tricked or duped.

Since a victim is someone who has been injured or destroyed, showing the cause of harm will provide part of his or her story's persuasive power. The story will alert its audience to the dangers to someone "like you and me" evident in the events it depicts. The mode of presentation, the very process of narrating character, desire, action, and consequence, promises to impart understanding. Relatability strategies ensure that explaining how and why someone became a victim extends warnings to its audience. Consequently, a victim's suffering gains meaning as sacrifice. We no longer have to throw anyone to the lions; we simply buy their life rights.

Within this rhetorical perimeter, a logic operates that further reinforces the persuasive power of a victim story. Victims suffer in the face of forces larger than themselves. Their lack of power, their relative helplessness, launches the process of their victimization and impels the telling of their story. Victims need witnesses to gain justice. An action, event, or circumstance can be confirmed as "wrong" as others besides victim and perpetrator come to know about it. Learning about a victim allows the means to respond to the helplessness that initiates their story. The existence of a wrong necessitates corrective action, creating the chain of events that will become the basis for the story's plot. When a witness tells about the victim, it exposes the process of victimization, bringing it to public light. The consequent awareness of dangers and the wrongs that have been committed creates the potential for remedies to arise.

Shannon Mohr is victimized through the abuse of courtship and marriage rituals, so that underlying her story's opposition of victim and perpetrator are the further oppositions of trust and duplicity, love and exploitation, and, of course, truth and lie. Dave Davis's successful entrapment of his victim in a marriage intended only to provide him with an insurance windfall allows him the opportunity to murder her and to appear innocent to law enforcement officials. Criminal concealment fosters victims; as survivors, these same victims enforce a process of investigative revelation. When wrongs have been committed, the logic of victimization turns to the responses necessary to bring harms to light in order to correct those wrongs.

The same logic also shows how Shannon Mohr is not the only victim harmed by Dave's intentions and systematic deceptions. To trust Dave is to become his victim. The greater the trust, the greater the harm. Alana, his first wife, left him after a beating she describes as Dave "blindsiding" her. Jeri Hobson, Dave's lover before and after he marries Shannon, goes to Florida with him and lives with him believing that Dave is a secret government operative and that Shannon has left him because of her involvement in a federal witness protection program.

Aside from Shannon herself, most harmed are Shannon's parents, Bob and Lucille Mohr, who entrust their daughter to Dave's vow to care for her "forever." The Shannon Mohr "story" becomes the story of their survival. Their role as parents/survivors is driven by the need to give their daughter's life meaning through bringing Dave Davis to justice for the wrongs he commits when he violates her trust and then profits from the violation.

Witness Logic

For all of Dave's victims, the film shows the process of providing witness as the logical response to victimization. Testimony mediates between victimization and whatever justice can do to remedy the harm. The investigation that occupies much of the film is given over to procedure (locating witnesses; convincing them to testify; accumulating enough testimony to establish a pattern of past deceptions). The testimony of witnesses would verify what has occurred, enabling a court of law to consider the criminal nature of the action. Davis, however, is able to deny or dissemble consistently what others have witnessed. His deceit is sufficiently skillful and systematic that he can delay the consequences of what others have seen him do or heard him say.

The logic of witnessing validates the persuasive claims regarding the need for justice, for moral and legal correction. Persuasion in *Mohr* tends to be particularly filmic. It presents the evidence afforded by key testimony through a Hitchcock-like manipulation of audience and character viewpoint. It builds persuasive argument through repeated and varied presentation of key actions (Davis's behavior), objects (a vial of chemical; Shannon's shoe), and statements (regarding Davis's past; the insurance policies covering Shannon; his claim she requested cremation). As viewers, we are aligned with everyone victimized by Davis's murder of Shannon Mohr. By sharing the film's overall narrative viewpoint, we too are positioned to desire that what we have seen will be shared externally and confirmed as public knowledge.

From its opening moments, *Mohr* makes clear how it will allocate the narrative viewpoint of witnesses within and outside of the diegesis. Over scenes of the wedding reception of one of Shannon's friends, the voice of Bob Mohr, Shannon's father, introduces Dave Davis to us as a man who "had come only to find someone to marry and murder." The voice-over/flashback configuration paints Davis as a liar and aligns the viewer with those in the story who know this. Relatable character desire (the desire to prove Davis's guilt) colors what we see as he courts his bride-to-be. The film's viewer subsequently witnesses Davis's lies. We see his action as duplicity; we know of his "true" intentions and inevitably "know" then that he is guilty of murder. His ability to dissemble, however, frustrates validating what we and characters within the film have witnessed.

From the premise that Davis acts only to deceive, we see him perpetrating several kinds of lies. He dissembles facts about his past, his current intentions, and his actions at the time of Shannon's fatal "accident."

As contradictions subsequently accumulate, the pattern of lying confirms the claim of premeditation made in the film's opening voice-over narration.

Davis's lies turn friends (Dick, a neighbor) and family (Bob and Lucille Mohr; Tracy, one of Shannon's cousins) into witnesses motivated to provide testimony. Davis builds a friendship with Dick, a Vietnam vet, with stories of his own combat tour in Vietnam. He shows the scar on his back from a shrapnel wound. At Shannon's funeral, however, Davis's mother tells Bob Mohr that her son never served. When this comes up later, while Dick is questioning Davis about other inconsistencies in what he's said and the way he's acted, Davis asserts that he was a covert operative and that the government will deny any record of his service.[27]

Foreshadowing occurs through initially marking and then accumulating contradictions. As Davis and Shannon drive up to his farm, their new home, he assures his new bride that he "insures you, me, everything." The property is smaller than what he'd led her to believe it might be. He does have enough money for the horses that he shows her he's bought as their wedding present. The scene marks horses and insurance as key elements of his duplicity.

Later, Dick is standing with Davis in the hospital corridor, when state police begin to investigate what happened. Davis tells them he has no insurance for Shannon. Shannon had told her parents, however, that she was insured. Davis then remembers that "there might be a small policy." He tells Dick the next day that he misunderstood, that he "thought they were asking about health insurance."

The morning of her death, Shannon and Davis argue about her parents coming to visit. As Davis urges the Mohrs to leave, Shannon stands behind him mouthing to her mother the words "Don't go." Davis insists he and Shannon go for a ride to work things out. We see them ride off; the next shot is Davis, galloping furiously up to Dick—Shannon's had an accident, she's "fallen off her horse," and he needs help getting her to the hospital. There Davis attempts to embrace Lucille Mohr. She withdraws, raising her hand to note the bloody scratches on his cheek.

As she hears (and rejects) Davis's statements about insurance and cremation, a near full fade to white initiates her brief flashback to that morning, and to Shannon urging her parents not to leave. Full color quickly returns. "It's all wrong," Lucille Mohr declares.

When he tells his same story to the state police, images flash back to the accident Davis describes. She falls. We see him drag her from the woods to the edge of a field. When Dick shows the state police the spot where the fall apparently occurred, he finds on the ground one of Shannon's unlaced shoes. If she fell off her horse, he asks, what is her shoe doing here, with the lace untied?

The film's construction of witnessing—its allocation of evidence about the murder through aural and visual emphasis and accumulating contradictions—shifts the narrative point of view and the burden of proof from the central witnesses (Dick; the Mohrs) to law enforcement and the media. As investigators in the media and law enforcement acquire knowledge and evidence, they come to share the frustration that began with the Mohrs. Brooks, the district attorney's chief investigator, "knows" (like everyone else) that Davis is guilty; however, he can gather only circumstantial proof, and then it takes a decade to catch Dave Davis. The validation of what everyone sees and "knows" is frustrated because of evasion and delay.

The ultimate result of this narrative movement outward from family is to shift the process of witnessing to two social institutions—the TV viewing audience and "the People"—as their interests are represented by the prosecution in criminal court. These shifts complete moving the investigation into the public realm, referring story events to the larger public in which we, as viewers, reside.

To break the pattern of frustrated witness (and to try to track down Davis, who has been a fugitive for ten years), Brooks has the idea of turning the case into an episode of *Unsolved Mysteries*. The move sets up a logical culmination of witness logic in the film. Throughout, in order to validate what people have seen, it has been necessary to use the media to shift what has been witnessed from private to public ownership. The media become involved in the investigation of Shannon's death after an initial inquiry demanded by the Mohrs does not lead to further police investigation. A reporter interviews Davis's first wife, Alana. Davis remains at large, and so the media also become frustrated investigators. It is not the first but a second airing of the *Unsolved Mysteries* episode that finally provides a tip resulting in Davis's capture. The textual reference anchors witnessing in actual, external media events. As TV program viewers provide primary evidence, witnessing gains the weight of media reality. Media presence warrants subsequent persuasive claims.

The program is more than a story event. The opening credits of the film explain that this movie-of-the-week is an *Unsolved Mysteries* production. Interviews with key figures punctuate the film at intervals, lending additional authority as self-contained commentary on important people

and action. Leger Grindon, in his discussion of *Reds,* describes how witness testimony there authenticates the narrative:

> Like the typical third-person narrator, the witnesses are not "embedded" in
> the diegesis; they remain outside the fictive world of the characters, but the
> authority of their commentary is based upon the fact that they were indeed
> part of that world—in fact, their experience takes precedence over the fiction
> itself . . . witnesses even give the impression that their recollections have guided
> and constrained the filmmakers in the construction of the fiction. In addi-
> tion, the witnesses combine the "voice of God" authority of a third-person
> narrator with the uncertainty of a first-person narrator. (218)

The interviews in *Mohr* are eventually explained as re-creations of the
Unsolved Mysteries program material when we see the show's crew prepar-
ing to interview the Mohrs in their living room. Since one purpose of
Unsolved Mysteries is to use reality TV to generate a sense of viewer involvement in the creation of an entertainment product, the TV show extends
participation in the investigation to program viewers, much like the narrative structure of the film we are watching situates the viewer as a frustrated witness. As witness statements are made public, they gain presence
and accessibility. Presence in the media gives testimony further substance.

In order for what they have seen to have effect, then, the film's view is
that the testimony of the Mohrs and others must first reach the news media. From there it makes the power of their position more evident to law
enforcement. For the district attorney's investigation to succeed, it turns
to reality TV to reach an international audience of potential witnesses. The
culmination (and greatest substantiation) of witness logic, then, is the film
we are seeing.

In particular, the prosecutor's closing argument as a narration of the
murder invites its listeners to imagine events based now on the inferable
actions suggested by witness testimony, circumstantial evidence, and forensic evidence. Tracy, Shannon's cousin, has testified that Davis kept Pentactin, a paralyzing drug, in the refrigerator. In addition to trace evidence
of the drug, puncture marks on Shannon's wrist and shoulder, discovered
in the second exhumation of her body, suggest that she had been injected
twice, shortly before her death. Scratch marks on Davis's face were the
result, he claimed, of his efforts to get help for her.

To this point, Davis remains the only witness to what happened. The
prosecution's evidence has done what it can to rebut Davis's testimony. It
remains to place Shannon Mohr into the case as a witness. In his summa-

tion, the prosecutor finally constructs a version of the story alternative to Davis's. The summation offers a speculative but a "corrected"—"institutionalized"—flashback. It reasserts the flashback as a primary source of information outside the limits of any one witness's viewpoint. It is essentially a collective view of events, reanchored in a version of actuality that claims validity because it incorporates all the forensic and testimonial evidence the trial has gathered. Consequently, we are finally allowed to see what must have "really" happened. In this speculative flashback, Shannon and Davis tie up their horses in the woods and start to make love. The inference is drawn from the premise for the ride (they were going to smooth things over after their fight about the Mohrs' visit) and accounts for the untied shoe as well as her partially removed shirt. She struggles with him when he tries to inject her; he hits her to stun her so that he can give her a second, more effective injection. The thrust of the summation is that in the last moments of her life, she is fully aware of what is happening but helpless to do anything about it. Her dying close-up shows her watching the betrayal of her trust and love, witness to her own victimization.

The summation "fills in" the story by showing the crucial moment of the murder. As viewers of this speculative flashback, we see the victim in the same position we've been in throughout the film—as a helpless witness to the wrong being perpetrated. The guilty verdict clarifies and reinforces the sense that wrong can delay but not evade the workings of justice. The summation also suggests that there is a societal obligation to provide articulation when victims are incapable of speaking for themselves. Giving the victim(s) a voice through the courts and the media contributes to the sense in the film that moral order has been restored by means of the most appropriate apparatus.

Persuasive Claims

The relatability strategies that structure *Mohr*'s narrative culminate logically, as warrants should, in the claims the film will forward. The logic of victimization addresses the question of why the Shannon Mohr story is exemplary and suggests the value of what might be learned from it. Witness logic grows directly out of the process of victimization. It tells us why we should believe the story we are being told. Witnessing articulates and verifies the nature of the wrongs committed against the victim. The strategies of exemplification and articulation warrant narrative resolution that restores a sense of moral order in the world of the film.[28]

The *Mohr* story's relatability strategies show a viewing public why it has a stake in this story. The film argues that, much like Shannon Mohr herself, legal and moral order is vulnerable. The film depicts the nature of evil that exploits trust and love and that can benefit from the ease and effectiveness of lying. Justice as a corrective force is close to failing here. What forces truth and justice to work finally, the film suggests, is parents embracing their responsibility to their children. Without the Mohrs' perseverance, their daughter's story would never have come to light. Their example serves as a warning to parents to consider how extensive their obligations to their children need to be. The film's manner of presentation argues also for the validity of this story as docudramatic argument. It translates survival, trial, and closure configurations, the relatability strategies characteristic of MOW docudrama, through the visual power of witness logic, affirming the truth value of testimony. It anchors this logic in the national media agenda, using this actuality anchor as the premise for telling its story through the form of a movie-of-the-week. Docudrama narrative here can do even what a trial cannot, by affording to us a complete, accessible, visually reconstructed view of what "happened." By arguing that we accept the value of the story, the lessons it offers, and its assertion that since this is a true story, linked to media events, what we are seeing "really happened this way," *Shannon Mohr* also would argue that this story, like docudrama generally, offers us an opportunity for empowerment.

Cheerleading, Murder, and Media Mayhem

The lengthy title promises a great deal: These will be *The Positively True Adventures of the Alleged Texas Cheerleader-Murdering Mom.* Only the assertion that the story will present the underlying "truth" of a real-life event could make credible this unusual juxtaposition of cheerleading and murder. The headline montage opening the film, modeling the front pages of the Houston *Post* and the cover of *People,* not only roots the story in the culture and current events of the 1990s but also suggests that while the legal issues have been resolved, larger, underlying questions remain (see fig. 13). The actual incidents, the trial, and surrounding publicity invite asking the question, Why did *this* happen? How could anyone's sense of right and wrong allow something as wholesome and harmless as cheerleading to lead to such (even allegedly) monstrous extremes?

Rather than presenting its story as an isolated, anomalous incident, *The Positively True Adventures of the Alleged Texas Cheerleader-Murdering Mom,* in appropriate 1990s MOW spirit, offers a contemporary moral cautionary tale. In 1992, Wanda Holloway was tried and convicted for soliciting the murders of one of her daughter's classmates, Amber Heath, and

Amber's mother, Verna. The MOW docudrama based on these events re-presents them as the results of Wanda's quest to place her daughter on a successful career path. The film explores three reasons why the desire to succeed in this case went wrong. First, the constraints of suburban life invite viewing self-promotion, rather than accomplishment, as the route to success. Second, self-promotion creates the problematic moral perspective that allows crossing the lines between right and wrong, fantasy and reality, and legal and illegal action. Third, seeking achievement through self-promotion invites devil's bargains, most notably with the media. The news and entertainment media in this story strongly influence everyone's motives. While providing prisms that people here use to judge each other, the same media show themselves, quite directly, doing so. The thrust and structure of the film's argument then serve to shed light of self-examina-tion. By exposing its own impact, this work depicts not only how the media has exacerbated a loss of moral perspective but also how—through analysis, self-assessment, and humor—docudrama may allow some per-spective to be restored.

The Holloways, the Harpers, and Wanda's Vision of Success

Family life in a middle-class society small enough that an individual's repu-tation matters frames the strategies the film uses to invite its target audi-ence to find links with its characters. The strength and spectrum of the film's argument stem from Wanda's relatability as a character. Wanda fills the center of the story's social matrix.

Through her remarriage, the three interlaced units in her extended family consist of the Holloways (Wanda, her present husband, C. D. Holloway, and Shane and Shanna Harper, the children from Wanda's previous marriage); Tony Harper, Wanda's ex-husband, and his current wife; and Terry Harper, Tony's brother, and his wife, Marla. The Holloways live in a suburban ranch house very similar in style, size (moderate), and furnishings (modest) to the home of Verna Heath.

Characters tend to be crowded in scenes that recur in familial settings. Visual space becomes the staging ground for social pressures. This is most extreme in the confines of Terry and Marla's trailer, where they fight, see things, throw things, and so forth (see fig. 14). The Heath living room also bustles with many small children, while the Holloway dining room table sets up family discussions in which, for example, the topic of Shane's request for a truck takes a backseat to Shanna's campaign for a place on the cheerleading squad (see fig. 15). Here the entire family works on Shanna's ill-fated campaign posters. "Heath" problems tend to occupy those in the front seat of Wanda's Jeep, such as Shanna, after she's disqualified in her bid to be a cheerleader, and, subsequently, Terry, who meets with Wanda there several times to discuss hiring a "professional" to solve the problem of Verna. Over-the-shoulder framing and shot-reverse angle-shot editing further condense the front seat's already intimate space. In crosscut car scenes, Wanda and Verna counsel their daughters on success and failure.[29] Later, Wanda and Terry use the car seat as a setting to entrap each other. The film equates crowded space with constrained desires, graphically justifying characters' needs to be upwardly mobile.

Economic issues direct the relations between all the members of the Holloway/Harper families. Before the arrest and trial, the explicit concerns revolve around child support. In the first scenes of the story, Shane asks his mother for money. She tells him to ask his father. In the follow-up telephone call, Tony asks his ex-wife what she's doing with all the child support money he sends her. Before they hang up, they negotiate splitting the $320 cost of the rulers Wanda orders as campaign tokens in Shanna's bid to be a cheerleader. When she's told such favors will be "illegal" this year, and the argument that they've already paid for them falls on deaf ears, Wanda decides they'll use the rulers rather than paint stirrers as the sticks that hold up Shanna's campaign signs. This fatal error disqualifies Shanna. Later, as he's trying to sell off investments and assets to pay for Wanda's defense, her husband ("C.D.") Holloway mutters to himself, "I should have just paid for the damn paint sticks." Wanda's decision to get rid of Verna Heath brings her to her ex-brother-in-law. She believes Terry knows a hit man. Their secret sessions in the front seat of the Cherokee deal largely with money. To protect himself, Terry uses the issue of the cost of the hit and the schedule of payments that would be wisest to string her along so that the police can wire him and tape the negotiations.

Family allegiance becomes a costly commodity. Marla, Terry's wife, otherwise plagued by hallucinations of furry insects on her floors and body, is the only one wise enough to tell Terry that he's bartered the future love and respect of his niece in exchange for his own legal safety. Terry's loyalty to his family becomes one of the main issues in the last half of the film, when members of both families war over who can sell their life rights and for how much. Tony feels his brother is a traitor for going out on his own and selling out cheap to ABC; however, he attempts to use Terry's negotiations as leverage in his own deal. Shanna confronts Tony: "Did you sell my rights?" Only his own rights, he tells her, but she disbelieves him. "Mama says you're stealing—they're my rights; it's *my* story." Shane, who tends to stand next to his father and to dress like him, tries to defend Tony by pointing out to his sister that Wanda keeps taking child support money even though they haven't lived with her for the last two months. When Tony comments to his son, "She gets more like her mother everyday," Shane wisely notes, "It's their symbiotic relationship."

As he is working on one of his sister's campaign signs and engulfed by poster board and markers, Shane tries repeatedly to raise the question of how and when he'll be able to get money to buy a truck for school. His needs, he argues, are just as paramount as his sister's. Wanda rebuffs him, then orders him to leave—saying, "I don't want to look at you anymore"— if the boy can't put his mind and energy into his sister's campaign. He throws down his markers and leaves.

The moment illustrates not only the sources of tension but also the problematic values in the family. In the face of economic constraints, coercion defines the difference between family members helping each other achieve desires as opposed to trying to use each other to satisfy self-interest. Consequently, Wanda questions Shane's loyalty to his sister, Tony points out the lack of loyalty of his own brother, and Wanda seeks out Terry to be the instrument to fulfill her fantasies for her daughter.

Are Wanda's actions and desires other-directed or self-directed, or are the two synonymous? Is she doing everything for her daughter or for herself, or is there no difference? In an early scene around the Holloway dinner table, Wanda lays out Shanna's dream: Cheerleading is only the entry point in the route to upward mobility. It's a career move, the start of "building a portfolio." Qualifying to be a cheerleader now, while Shanna is in junior high, will allow her to be a cheerleader in high school. From there, she will be able to win a scholarship as a college cheerleader, and college will be her springboard to her successful career in acting, singing, and modeling. She will, Wanda tells C.D., be able to "buy you a bungalow."

This, of course, is Wanda talking, rather than Shanna. The tones of coercion and appropriation return several scenes later. After Shanna has endured the shame of disqualification, her mother consoles her with how "next year will be a whole new game." Shanna doesn't want to try out again; she's "sick of it." Wanda tells her coolly to go ahead and quit, to never mind eight years of hard work and all the money they've spent on her.

The psychology of Wanda as a stage mother who would induce her daughter to act out her own almost uncontainable desire for achievement remains one kind of issue. What is more important here is the element of self-promotion characteristic of the career and the vision of pursuing it. Wanda's notions of success raise the larger question of what the quality of a life based upon cheerleading might ultimately be. More immediately, cheerleading is never discussed as something done to fire up the fans at a game but instead is important because it will display Shanna publicly. Wanda's idea that effective public exposure determines "success" as an entertainer comes up in her first telephone conversation with her ex-husband. All Shanna needs to succeed, she tells Tony to convince him to help her split the cost of the investment, is a gimmick, some help in the task of promoting herself.

Verna Heath is a problem in Wanda's mind because she has been able to promote Amber effectively. At the conclusion of a gymnastics class, the instructor begins to talk to Verna and Amber; seeing this, Wanda puts her arm around Shanna, walks up and barges in ("Is my daughter giving you any trouble?"), ensuring that Shanna will also share the instructor's attention. When her plea to use the five hundred rulers is rejected, Wanda argues repeatedly that "last year Verna Heath had the rules bent to accommodate her." Her belief that Verna has engineered an unfair advantage for Amber becomes her spoken justification for what she does subsequently. "I've been shafted before, over and over," she tells one of her interviewers. "When I'm pushed, I push back."

She sees the competition between Amber and Shanna then as a contest between two mothers to see who can assert herself the most effectively. Her actions are as much "for" her daughter's vision of success as they are for her own sense of self-actualization. It envisions the mother role not entirely as self-sacrifice nor self-indulgence but as a fusion of both extremes, as if in the 1990s, Veda Pierce became a mother and decided she had to be a bit more like Stella Dallas.

"Good" People Get Promoted

Wanda's coercion of those around her to suit her own will and desires, to satisfy her vision of upward mobility, has limited effect outside her immediate family. As Wanda makes a series of bad judgments with increasingly problematic consequences, it becomes evident that she has placed self-promotion at the center of her scale of values and that she assumes that others operate the same way. She observes that others do worse things and are allowed to get away with them and consistently minimizes the implications of her own statements and actions. Her reluctance to accept personal responsibility results from her self-centered moral perspective.

To "succeed" in Wanda's system of values means to be a person of "quality." Wanda tells Shanna at the beginning of the film that "[Amber's] family's not quality, OK? 'Most she has to look forward to is marriage to a football player, who'll manage a Dairy Queen." Her response to Shanna's announcement that she is ready to quit trying to become a cheerleader—and Shane's brief efforts to support his sister—ends by informing them that she will brook "no low-rent nobodies, and it begins in this family." Since she treats Shane dismissively, only Shanna receives her help in becoming a "somebody." "Somebodies" are successes. Success comes through promotion.

Wanda's perspective on family "quality" and personal "success" becomes even more problematic when she tries to apply the same values outside her own family. Her blind desire for her daughter's success leads to a series of worsening transgressions. She decides it will be all right to use the rulers with "Shanna for Cheerleader" printed on them, even though she's asked and been told specifically that this will violate the rules. Her fantasy of getting rid of Verna and Amber as obstacles to her daughter's success leads her to ask Terry to set up a contract with a hit man. After she is arrested, her defense is based on her belief that all she did was to express that fantasy out loud, that it was a joke. Because of her arrest and trial, she and other members of her family attain the notoriety and even a bit of the wealth that she hoped would be Shanna's—and theirs—as a result of cheerleading. Wanda goes on national talk shows and becomes the subject of a movie-of-the-week. The lines blur between good and poor judgment, reality and fantasy, legal and illegal action, and fame and infamy, because she has defined right and wrong in terms of self-gain. Through the film's depiction of these progressively corrupt fantasies, we are offered an answer to the question of "why this happened." We are shown the limits and risks inherent in a moral perspective derived from Wanda's typically 1990s sense of what it takes to succeed.

The story's relatability strategies, its rooting in everyday limits and aspirations, invite asking how close any of us are to crossing these lines. The case foregrounds the moral implications of fantasy bleeding over into action when cultural values arguably support Wanda Holloway's kind of self-centered scheme of right and wrong.

Media Mayhem

The film also offers an answer to the question of what the sources are of a vision of success based on self-promotion. Recurring references to Gulf War news items not only establish the story's setting but also implicitly compare individual and national policies of acting on the basis of perceived best self-interest. Throughout the film, the role and function of the media are integral to this suggested culture of self-promotion that frames Wanda's vision of success.

Media are constantly present in the film, as on-screen agents and as narrative devices. Media indicate the means of self-actualization for characters by showing these individuals ways to fulfill their potentials in life. The media ultimately provide the perspectives through which characters judge events, themselves, and each other.

The idea that characters view the media as a means of self-actualization inheres within Shanna's ambition. The same culture has created the Dallas Cowboy cheerleaders. Wanda's concept of career preparation (cheerleading leads to singing, acting, and entertaining) assumes that the media are essential to attaining these desires, that image and self-promotion are means to attain self-worth, and that stardom provides a position of social power. Media exposure as a means of fulfillment becomes the order of the day once everyone tries to exploit the publicity resulting from Wanda's trial.

Two comparable scenes show Shanna's changing status at school. In the first, right after she's been disqualified, Shanna leans against her locker, isolated, taunted by a group of girls (with Amber in the center) across the way. Others gossip and laugh at her. Later, just before the trial, Shanna walks down the same corridor, surrounded by admirers. Now Amber is alone, across the corridor, standing under a sign ("Vote for Amber Heath") with concentric red target circles painted over her name (see fig. 16). Clearly, Shanna's newfound popularity is a result of the fact that now she and her mother are famous.

On the morning the trial is to begin. everyone stands in appropriate groups on the sidewalk outside the courthouse. Tony and his wife arrive in a chauffeured limousine. Tony is talking to someone on a cell phone. Tony has been involved in selling family photographs and life rights negotiations, so the visual implication is that he has gone "Hollywood" (see fig. 17). Terry stands by himself, at some distance from all factions, leaning against a tree, his spatial isolation reflecting how his family regards him as the turncoat who framed Wanda and, even worse, that he is traitorously attempting to strike up a movie deal on his own.

The media here provide images for characters to aspire to; in addition, the media structures provide the shape and texture of the story the film is telling us. The "present" of this film is an interview Wanda Holloway is granting, Shanna beside her, to the producers of the film we are seeing. The interview is presented in ten brief segments dispersed throughout the film. Temporal cuts to the events we are being told about reveal the rest of the story. The shotgunned interview, recalling documentary practice, allows comparisons and contrasts within the material to emerge. The interplay allows a balancing of perspectives. We are afforded a larger view of Wanda's perceptions. For example, in the third interview segment, she characterizes Terry as having "been shady, a different sort of person, not one of us." The next scene shows Terry approaching Mike, his friend at work, with his "five-year plan" for self-improvement. He's going to give up drugs, drink, smoking, improve financially, and "get more stability" in his personal life. His resolutions confirm that he may have been "shady" but also suggest he's trying to change. The juxtaposition shows that Wanda's judgment of Terry is partially correct but limited. She tells her interviewer that she no longer plays the piano in church but is very "family oriented." The film flashes back to her at the keyboard in church, followed by the first scene at her home, on the phone, arguing about child support with Tony. Again, the strategy includes but surpasses what she says, providing additional perspective beyond what Wanda sees herself. The comparisons and contrasts allow us to understand that the value Wanda places on self-promotion is a logical consequence of her self-centered perceptions. Perhaps the most telling interview excerpt precedes the two scenes that show her desire to get rid of Verna Heath shifting from an impulsive fantasy to a premeditated act. She tells her interviewer, "There's nothing wrong with competition as long as you can keep it where it belongs. Because of what was coming at Shanna, I had to keep pushing from my side." At that point, however, nothing is "coming at Shanna," and "pushing" involves stating out loud in front of her children her wish for Verna's death. We then see Wanda contemplating a sign bearing the symbol of a drowning swimmer, followed by her first contact with Terry to set up the hit. She acts not for Shanna but for herself. This is no longer Shanna's desire but Wanda "pushing back" because she has not obtained what she wants for her daughter.

The film's flashback/interview structure renders the narration from Wanda's viewpoint and also shows the large extent to which this is a story about the media. Wanda's "story"—Wanda herself—becomes difficult to distinguish from media constructions. The Heaths, Holloways, and Harpers live in Channelview, Texas. Wanda's use of and use by the media allow her self-definition by means of public attention, the form of stardom she has attained. She can create self-image through her media image. Wanda's interview comments reflect denial and self-absorption, even as they progress from self-assessment ("I can't do anything right") to judgment of others (Terry has "been shady, a different sort of person, not one of us") to judgment of her verdict (she can't believe she was sentenced to "fifteen years for this one little thing"; people are "going to look at [her] like [she's] a freak for the rest of her life"). In the last interview sequence, she has asked the interviewer for his opinion. He replies, off camera, "I suppose what I feel is that you did wrong; ultimately, you did wrong." She thinks for a moment, then is allowed a final self-justification: "Everybody needs a scapegoat."

The film's media presence becomes a key channel of narration. By the time of the trial, the last major crisis, the news media narrate events to characters within the story. Wanda turns to the media for its presentation and assessment of her as the trial phase begins; since we are fed her story from her point of view, much of the last half of the film shows us Wanda, often seated next to Shanna, watching herself in news reports and on talk shows. A local news story about the arrest gives way to *Life* magazine and *Current Affair* photographers and producers lurking on the Holloway and Heath front doorsteps. During the trial, news coverage tells Wanda bluntly that her defense is "crumbling." She watches herself give an interview, using national airtime to apologize to Verna and ask her forgiveness. One night during the trial, Wanda and C.D. channel surf from Johnny Carson making a joke about her to other talk show stand-up routines doing the same thing. Just as Shanna has benefited from her newfound fame at school, Wanda's life is becoming fully illuminated by the light of the media.

The presence of the media within the story leads logically to the film presenting its own processes of inception and creation. The framing interview is left in a "rough" outtake form, retaining calls to makeup, problems with the microphone, and a floor assistant tripping while trying to scurry off camera, which elicits laughs from the Holloway women. We see this production company vie with others, as well as with producers from the likes of *Current Affair,* for the time and life rights of the principals. In one scene, Tony and Terry haggle in a restaurant restroom over how to sell their rights. Shortly afterward, the writer for the production company that will make the film we are seeing hears that a writer for a competitor affiliated with ABC has offered more money to Terry. She responds by saying, "Never believe what a writer tells you." A few scenes later, as she is walking with Verna, discussing the prospective casting for the project, the same writer expresses the belief that Holly Hunter will be right for the part of Wanda. The credit roll verifies that the film's writer has played herself in these scenes.

Through its self-conscious view of the media's influence on people and events, the film overcomes offering an involuted, strictly self-directed examination of its material in order to broach external issues of responsibility. By the end of the film, Terry Harper, perhaps the only character throughout who has appeared to question his own reasons for doing things, understands that one impact of media-induced prominence in his life is that his dilemmas have shifted from issues of self-protection to those of self-promotion. He asks a coworker, from whom he's solicited advice all through the film, whether it is "immoral for me to sell my rights for something that was immoral to begin with?" His friend thinks for a second and answers, "I don't know," probably as most of us would.

As Wanda's last exchange with her interviewer makes emphatic, she has consistently maintained that her posture has been to push back, that she views her actions as standing up for her daughter and herself. The focus on Wanda's viewpoint leaves room for judgment as to why she *went* wrong, as well as how she may *be* wrong. The film takes a presentational, rather than rigidly judgmental, posture toward its depiction of how and when Wanda's fulfillment of her role as mother crosses lines of acceptability. The film allows the possibility of reading Wanda as a product of the pressures of her role, suggesting that women can be made crazy by the expectations placed upon them as wives and mothers. The glimpses the film offers of Verna Heath ultimately support this. Small children fill scenes of her home. Her response to the *Current Affair* producer who asks if he can do anything is to send him out for food for all the kids inside the house. She deals with the news that Wanda has taken out a contract on her by continuing to put away children's toys. The last scene of the film is perhaps most telling in placing a "cheerleading mom" in context: The marching band rehearses "Stars and Stripes Forever" while Verna sits alone in the vastness of the bleachers, coaching Amber, also by herself down on the field, through cheerleading routines. The band quits, the lights in the empty stadium are struck, the camera begins a slow zoom back so that the American flag fills the foreground, and Verna's order of "Go back to the beginning" echoes throughout the sudden silence. Verna's compulsion has survived everything that's happened, unchanged. The madness continues.

Elayne Rapping argues that TV movies-of-the-week tend to valorize the images of women because they both address and present women's viewpoints (64). This film suggests a qualification of the idea that viewpoint and valorization are synonymous; it offers alternatively a spectrum of the constraints on its characters, contextualizing the Harper brothers' contrasting ambitions, or the factors that drive cheerleading moms to abnormal extremes.

The film's view of media responsibility strikes the same kind of balance. The film goes to lengths to expose the role of the media in general and its own contribution in particular to pushing characters past boundaries of decency, duty, and loyalty. It often does so with a distinct element of play-fulness. The film shows a two-way street, in which the media and its sub-ject/players seek each other out and use each other. The film's humor ex-tends the fault for weak individuals, easily led astray by the temptations of prominence, to other institutions that have difficulty dealing with lives complicated by media presence. Wanda's lack of perspective is not helped by the fallibilities of an educational institution that turns cheerleader try-outs into full-fledged political campaigns but is, as we see it here, espe-cially ineptly handled by legal institutions, by the police and the courts. The police are shown as bumblers: They can't get a microphone to stick to a telephone receiver, and the image of Terry, in the front seat of a car with his arms up, shirt off, being wired by a police technician with his face up against Terry's chest, is incongruously sexual. A cop clumsily knocks over a stack of tapes on his desk, eliciting a panicked, hysterical scream from poor Verna, who has otherwise appeared to be in control in the face of the evidence that Wanda has ordered up her murder. When Wanda is arrested and asks if jewelry would be appropriate to wear in jail, one of the detectives turns and mutters to himself, "God, I miss drug busts," sug-gesting that he has fallen some distance in carrying out his job. Lawyers in the film don't fare much better. Wanda's lawyer looks like he's going to be sick when Marla, one of their key witnesses, has to admit under cross-examination that she takes medication because she tends to see "furry things" everywhere. As he tries to give his summation, Wanda's attorney is pushed aside by a court bailiff and then interrupted by the judge, who instructs him to "wind it up," as if this whole affair has wasted enough of the court's time.

By exposing elements of the absurdity of the arrest, trial, and resulting publicity, the film implies that perhaps a mountain has been made of a molehill, and that very fact may be the "story" here. As much as Wanda may be at fault for her excesses and Terry for his weakness in the face of his ex-sister-in-law, each institution the story touches upon also can be faulted for allowing itself to be used for petty purposes—family and school, for providing a platform for Shanna's "dream"; the courts for bringing Wanda's corrupt fantasies to light and defining them as criminal; and the media, for allowing that light to appear so bright and rewarding.

The film maintains a balanced, presentational stance, suggesting that even its own exploitation can be enlightening. Individuals in the world it depicts receive little help from their culture in maintaining perspective on the differences between selflessness and self-indulgence, fame and infamy, right and wrong, and what it means to deserve "success." The film places its own work within this process, so that its storytelling acts as a restorative. It argues that one good docudrama can do is to provide a means for some regained, necessary perspective during times when cheerleading leads to murder and media mayhem.

In Media Veritas?

By their foregrounding of witnessing as a means of historical record, and promoting an awareness of their own processes of constructing discourse, *Shannon Mohr* and *The Positively True Adventures of the Alleged Texas Cheerleader-Murdering Mom* remind us that perhaps the most basic purpose of docudrama is, as the very name suggests, to dramatize documents.

In these works, media presence provides the persuasive premise for their stories. The chain of logic that results connects the known with the true. The facts of a news story, its data, have appeared on the public agenda. They anchor the resulting narrative to the actual materials at their source. This warrants docudramatic re-creation, making the case for the validity of the view of events the work presents, its persuasive claim. Just as *JFK* underlines the printed and filmic documents that are a major part of its subject matter, MOW docudramas situate their subjects in cultural discourse when they signpost their sources in news coverage and other forms of published, contemporary history.[30]

TCMM and *Mohr,* in particular, illustrate how the presence of the media can function in ways that are very similar and, at the same time, fundamentally very different in MOW docudrama. Media presence in both films warrants their shared assertion that what we see in these stories "really happened" this way.

If I Know about It, It Must Be True . . .

The death of Shannon Mohr was transformed from local news to a national audience participation event when it was broadcast as an episode of the reality TV program *Unsolved Mysteries.* The foibles of Wanda Holloway became immediate national news. In both cases, the prominence of the news stories lent credence to the MOW narratives that resulted. Status as news elevates people and events from the private to the public realm, establishing the parameters of public knowledge within which docudramatic re-creation can operate.

Information that undergoes the transformation from news to docudrama story comes with preestablished authority. Its legitimacy is not an issue because its provenance has been verified. What has been on the public agenda is acceptable, communal information, ready to function as shared knowledge and experience in a long form narrative.[31] It is not surprising, then, to find *Mohr* and *TCMM* foregrounding their origins by re-creating the media material at the sources of their stories. These materials include re-created interviews that structure both narratives and give them a documentary "feel," as well as the programs that present the interview material. Both *Mohr* and *TCMM* as narratives reveal the oppositions inherent within the process of docudramatization (the told vs. the untold; the explicit vs. the implicit; events as "found" vs. events as "produced"; etc.).

Both films begin with interview segments that recur as their stories develop. The *Mohr* interviews[32] appear complete, finished, each allowing key figures to present unchallenged narrative information. No other filmic elements appear to contradict or counterpoint interview statements. They remain unchallenged, infallible, integral parts of the larger narrative project. As breaks from and contributions to the narrative, the interview segments validate the priority of the testimony they present.

The shotgunned segments re-creating alleged Texas cheerleader-murdering Wanda Holloway's interview with the producer of the film we eventually will be watching maintain their "unfinished" nature indicating their status as part of a creative process. We see Wanda's appearances on a number of programs and as the subject of numerous newspaper and magazine articles. The segments accumulate, and as they counterpoint pertinent narrative scenes, the film's assertions about characters and events arise through the building interrelations of action and interview segments.

The incorporation of re-created media materials contributes substantially to the sense of each work presenting an "inside view" of its events. The *Mohr* interviews, for their part, are portrayed as the results of the desire of the central characters to see justice succeed. The TV program and this resulting MOW serve this desire. The works advocate for the victim. By remaining finished and unchallenged, interview testimony can contribute to the Mohrs' (and the story's) larger goal of restoring moral and legal order in the world of the film. The TV program is re-created with the docudrama. Narrative rupture is not an issue.

The *TCMM* interviews and varied media program materials, on the other hand, offer statements by the victim. Testimony, rather than remaining closed and finished, is open and ongoing, so that the interviews also provide information to which the interview subject responds ("Did I do wrong?" Wanda asks her interviewer). The combined shotgunned interview segments, talk show appearances, print articles, dramatic sequences, and concern for other production companies competing for the

Holloways' life rights not only comment on Wanda's story but also direct reference to the production of discourse outside the narrative.

Both films depict the media acknowledging the importance of its own role. In *Mohr,* the media validates itself by confirming the effect of public participation it has elicited in the story events. The film spawned by the program and re-creating its success is self-congratulatory.

TCMM validates the media by showing it questioning its own functions. It suggests the full run of Wanda Holloway's problems are the result of the impact of the media on our concepts of fame and the necessity of self-promotion to succeed in contemporary society. By exposing its own role, it suggests further that awareness may lead to solution. And what better way is there to create necessary awareness than a docudrama that shows the consequences of what one's life can be worth if value is defined solely by media marketability?

In both cases, the media acknowledges the importance of its own role in presenting narrative information. We are left with two very different styles of asserting docudramatic truth, one that is traditional and self-contained and the other that is externally referential and self-conscious. These contrasting works share common features: narrative structures that foreground their origins in established media presentations; resulting docudramatic re-creation that offers an "inside" view of these known events; and arguments for the importance of the presence of media in our lives.

6 | Recent Feature Film Docudrama as Persuasive Practice

After 1995, television networks and cable outlets de-emphasized their commitment to MOW docudrama production.[1] On the other hand, the mid- to late-1990s saw an unabated surge in the distribution of feature film docudramas. If works such as *JFK, In the Name of the Father,* and *Schindler's List* indicated the strength of the early-1990s market for features based on true stories, the same market showed little sign of slacking off approaching the end of the decade. The first two months alone of 1999 supported the continuing runs of *A Civil Action* (Steven Zaillan) and *At First Sight* (Irwin Winkler); the critical successes of *Hilary and Jackie* (Anand Tucker) and *October Sky* (Joe Johnston); and the remarkable profitability of *Patch Adams* (Tom Shadyac).[2] The year's end saw not only the releases of *Music of the Heart* (W. Craven) and *Girl, Interrupted* (J. Mangold) but also academy award attention turned to *The Insider* (Michael Mann) and *The Hurricane* (N. Jewison).

It remains to be determined if this sustained interest in feature film docudrama may be due in part to the producers of theatrical films following the lead of MOW creators in seeking out material that is rootable, relatable, and promotable. Inherent differences between MOWs and features in production scheduling and market strategies suggest very different needs for product promotion. Since filmmakers, unlike MOW producers, are freed from thinking in terms of "sweeps" periods, they have, in fact, the luxury of equating rootability and promotability. If a work is "based on a true story," its roots in reality logically become one of the main points in its promotion. Certainly the late-1990s have seen a turn toward features that, much like their MOW relatives, tend toward treating one person's life story as a model of empowerment. In any case, the extent to which product promotability is important to film docudrama producers is outside the scope of this study. Assuming that MOW and feature film docudramas—as stories—appeal to their respective audiences for similar reasons, the basic purpose here is to determine if recent feature film docudrama shows evidence of the same kind of relatability strategies that characterize MOW docudrama.

Previous chapters have examined how the telling of stories "based on actual events" in either medium creates relatability through identification and exemplification, resulting in arguments by example. Docudrama form creates a framework for relatability by converting the character/conflict/ closure structure of the classic Hollywood narrative film into melodramatic configurations of victim, trial, and articulation. The MOW propensity to tell stories of victims, the trials they undergo, and to articulate the moral implications of their survival becomes equally evident in the feature film docudramas of the late 1990s. The iconography of victim and trial in these films, however, creates relatability, as the films explore victimization through issues of work, family, race, and law. The choice of "real stories" to tell also warrants the films' basic persuasive purpose: to instruct their audiences as they clarify moral values at stake in the worlds they depict.

The 1997 Feature Film Docudramas

During 1997, a group of no less than six feature film docudramas reached American movie theaters. Christmas 1996 saw the openings of *Shine* (Scott Hicks), *Ghosts of Mississippi* (Rob Reiner), and *The People Vs. Larry Flynt* (Milos Forman). Subsequently, these shared their runs with three more features based on true stories, beginning with the winter release of *Rosewood* (John Singleton), followed shortly by *Donnie Brasco* (Mike Newell). The year ended with the pre-Christmas release of *Amistad* (Steven Spielberg).

In addition to appearing close together in time, the topography of the group displays some basic rhetorical common ground. Taken together, the stories address issues of law, family, and/or race. The narratives in *Brasco, Flynt,* and *Shine* center on finding justice in the pursuit of work; each of the other three (*Ghosts, Rosewood,* and *Amistad*) tell of a quest for justice in matters of race. The main characters of *Flynt, Brasco,* and *Shine* are exemplary because they are all driven by their work. Their stories consider the impact of family and law on their professional accomplishments. Family concerns also affect the search for equal racial justice that becomes the work of the main characters in *Ghosts, Rosewood,* and *Amistad.* The two subgroupings of films employ similar, docudramatic persuasive strategies in arguing that their subjects are exemplary and that we, as their audience, should learn from their examples. Below the topics that present the visible surfaces of their stories, the films, as docudramas, reveal the same kind of narrative structure evident in MOW docudramas. These late-1990s features, however, depart from their MOW cousins on matters of characterization, ideology, and arguments for empowerment.

First, these films depict male main characters melodramatically, presenting the stories of male, rather than female, victims. This holds true even in the case of *Ghosts of Mississippi,* which ostensibly shows us Myrlie Evers's search for justice in the murder of her husband, Medgar. At bottom, each story claims to be exemplary because it tells of self-sacrifice. The first subgroup of films argues that we should view their main characters as martyrs because of their willingness to sacrifice themselves for their work. Work emerges from these stories as paradoxical, an ongoing balance of cost and accomplishment. The men of the second subgroup give themselves over to the struggle for racial equality. Narrating their stories raises fundamental matters of story ownership and appropriation. In each film, the problem of whose story serves most effectively arises as a consequence of learning about how justice functions in matters of race.

Second, as male-centered stories, the films show ideological constraints to be not simply destructive but (ironically) self-destructive. While the victims may confront specific, individual antagonists, it becomes clear in each story that they must survive the harms of repressive ideologies that perpetuate and exacerbate injustice. The conflicts growing out of ideological constraints culminate in literal or figurative trials.

Third, as MOWs often make evident, surviving a trial constitutes victory as much as does receiving a favorable verdict. "Mere" survival becomes an argument for empowerment. To reinforce how survival is a form of victory, articulation scenes that clarify the moral issues the films have argued bring their stories to closure. *Rosewood* and *Amistad* will serve to detail how, as a consequence of offering arguments by example, these films also pose different answers to the fundamentally docudramatic question of story ownership.

Donnie Brasco, The People Vs. Larry Flynt, Shine

The victims of work. In each of these films, the action tends to center on the work of the main character. Work provides and takes away, makes men and consumes them. Work creates each man's identity and also becomes the source of their victimization because it demands self-sacrifice.

Donnie Brasco is really Joe Pistone, an undercover police officer who infiltrates a mob family and spends years playing the role of one its foot soldiers. Larry Flynt publishes *Hustler* magazine. David Helfgott is an artist, an aspiring concert pianist. The stories share a common thread:

Work becomes the very essence of each man's being. Work defines who they are and why they exist and determines how they are vulnerable.

Donnie Brasco makes work central because it begins from the premise that criminal activity is an every day job. Stuart Klawans notes that

> [a]lthough these new mobsters are supposed to be operating at the end of the seventies, they seem more like nineties working stiffs, pushed relentlessly to be more productive. The boss demands his profit; the underlings grind it out.[3] (35)

Donnie is one of the best of these stiffs. Pistone can function as a cop only if he is good at being a crook. Pistone, like Flynt and Helfgott, is victimized by embracing his work and succeeding. The depth of his infiltration of the mob is unprecedented. His "Brasco" persona ultimately provides invaluable, never-before attained information that eventually helps convict hundreds of Mafia figures. The subjects of *Flynt* and *Shine* work with comparable focus, dedication, and effectiveness. Larry Flynt rises from childhood Kentucky poverty by capitalizing (with eventually spectacular success) on his clientele's appetite for vice. He finds that to continue in his labor of exploiting the human body, he must become a defender of human rights. *Shine* examines how David Helfgott as a noted young concert pianist becomes driven in his training by the goal of performing Rachmaninoff's *Piano Concerto No. 3*. Preparation that focuses only on art does not sustain him when he must relate to an audience. His psyche is constructed, nearly destroyed, and reconstructed around his opportunities to communicate as an artist.

In each case, we see the results of the compulsion to work at all costs. Their stories depict the men as contemporary martyrs, willing to sacrifice their lives for the sake of the principles and goals of what they do. The films convey the element of sacrifice as a matter of suffering visible in the surface ripples of a story (we see how key relationships suffer because of the need to work) that eventually reveals underlying currents, the ideological contradictions creating deeper disturbances.

In all three stories, the main characters' professional pursuits jeopardize key domestic relationships. In essence, work puts love at risk. Since the films are (in part) melodramas, settings come to reflect the destructive conflicts growing out of work issues. In *Brasco*, for example, consecutive kitchen scenes convey the growing opposition between Joe Pistone's marriage and his friendship, as Donnie Brasco, with Lefty, the mobster who has become his *patrone*. The scenes equate spatial proximity with personal involvement. At Christmas, Donnie tries to drop off Lefty's present while he is on his way home to his real family. He stays for dinner. Much of what we see of the evening occurs while Donnie, and Lefty's wife and son, crowd into the kitchen to join Lefty while he cooks dinner (see fig. 18). In contrast to this cozy scene, Joe arrives at his own home so late that the house seems empty. He begins to rearrange the contents of the cupboards, continuing the idea that men belong in their kitchens. His wife comes down from bed; his young daughters have gone to stay with friends for the night. They have the first of increasingly heated fights about his absence from home. The argument turns to frantic lovemaking on the stairway. The next scene reiterates his growing alienation from his real family. Joe fixes breakfast for his two girls who have little to say to him. The resolution of this contrast between the "close" as opposed to "distant" scenes of the two men in their respective kitchens is to show them the next day, framed side by side in the front seat of Donnie's Cadillac, comfortably discussing their work.

A comparable progression of master bedroom scenes shows the impact of work on the compatibility of Larry and Althea Flynt's marriage. The film depicts Althea as a soul mate and an integral part of Flynt's work in running his *Hustler* organization. In their first home, the master bedroom looks like something out of a Western whorehouse, with glimpses of garish colors, huge hot tubs, and mounted animal heads accentuating the decor. As Flynt's empire and influence grow, they move to a Los Angeles mansion with its own unique decor, with the addition of barred windows and retractable armored shutters. Flynt is shot and paralyzed defending in court his right to work. He spends months locked away in the bedroom while Althea nurses him. She injects him with painkillers; as he sinks back into the stupor of the morphine, she joins him in this venture as well, tying off her arm and finishing the syringe. Flynt drops the drugs after surgery alleviates his constant pain, but Althea's dependency and deterioration prove fatal. Her devotion to remaining a companion to Flynt, along with Flynt's devotion to the "cause" created by his work, wreak irrevocable physical damage to them both and eventually make him a widower. The ending of the film, also set in the Flynts' bedroom, underlines what the cost of Flynt's work has been.

Shine associates parental control with confining living space and images of water. The Helfgott's house has small rooms, narrow hallways, and a fenced-off yard. David's father, Peter Helfgott, simultaneously supports and suppresses David's musical training because of his need to control his family. He trains the very young David to compete in contests that would win the boy opportunities to travel and study elsewhere but wants to deny those chances to David because it means his son will leave home. David pursues his possibilities; one day he receives a letter informing him he has won a scholarship to study in America. David's sisters urge their brother to read the letter out loud. As their pleasure increases in the letter's description of what David will do when he comes to study in the United States, Peter can no longer tolerate any of it. He tears the letter from his son's hand, crumples it into a ball, and throws it into the wood stove. Distraught, David walks to his teacher's front door, but no one answers his knock. He sinks down to sit on the doorstep; a close-up of his tear-streaked face is cut to a close shot of water dripping from the bathtub faucet at home (see fig. 19). His father enters the bathroom. Apparently, Peter is to take over the tub of hot water, but, as he comments in a still neutral tone of voice, David has "shit in the water, what a disgusting thing to do." He begins to beat the boy with his towel, violently spraying the bath water everywhere. Despite, or perhaps because of, his father, the next section of the film finds David in school in England. Here he studies with Cecil (Ralph Richardson), a one-handed master who, in one scene, seats David on the bench next to him so that the student can provide the other hand to the piece, literally becoming a physical extension of the teacher.

Psychologically, David continues to be a product of patriarchal controls over his life. When David leaves, his father states that he "has no son." David's pursuit of his calling as a concert pianist has cost him as well as liberated him from his relationship with his father. The film systematically associates water with the "breaks" in David's persona and circumstances; like the spray from Peter's towel, huge close-ups of drops of sweat rain from his face and hair during his collegiate recital of the Rachmaninoff piano concerto, just before he suffers the nervous breakdown that derails his career for a decade; we also see him standing in the rain, peering through the window at Moby's, the wine bar where he will walk in, begin to play, resume a career, and meet his future wife, who lives by the sea (see fig. 20). Before, water was associated with the harmful repression of David's desire to work; now and subsequently, the film's water motif suggests rebirth.

Joe Pistone, Larry Flynt, and David Helfgott all see important relationships in their lives changed because of their needs to work. As a further consequence, each man becomes victimized by the very ideological system that should sustain them and the work they are attempting to accomplish. Each film points in a different way to the destructive and ironic nature of patriarchy. Larry Flynt depends upon the First Amendment to allow him to publish a magazine that appeals to the basest kind of male chauvinism; however, the film suggests that defending that right in court consumes much of his working life. It is, of course, when he is walking out of a courthouse in the midst of one of the several trials that occupy him that he is shot. As a paraplegic, he becomes a pornographer deprived of a normal sex life. In his role as an undercover cop, Pistone is forced to be a criminal. He is out there alone, in constant danger of discovery. His FBI colleagues appear ill equipped to help him effectively. Ultimately, Pistone's FBI career ends when Brasco's job is finished. His job creates an intolerable dilemma: As Pistone, he must compromise his obligations to his wife; as Brasco, he must eventually betray Lefty, who has become a surrogate father to him in the mob family. Caught in a comparable double bind, David Helfgott's devotion to music is ignited by his father, who then tries to contain just how brightly the flame should "shine." The Helfgott family's rigid patriarchy reflects Peter's own upbringing (and loss of his family) during the Holocaust; Peter's desire to control fate by keeping his family together now becomes, ironically, the crushing weight of repression that devastates his son. He repeatedly makes David listen to and complete with him the story of the violin he saved to buy when he was a boy, and how his father took it away and smashed it. As one critic put it, "By their final confrontation, when his father is near death and David— a mental wreck—refuses to supply the payoff, we realize the significance of the metaphor. In their relationship, David himself has been the violin" (Rayner 116).

In these films, characters who act as antagonists—the other FBI agents in *Brasco,* the court opponents and the anonymous assassin in *Flynt,* even Peter in *Shine*—are transparent emblems of the systems of law and patriarchy that oppose the protagonists' desires. Antagonism here tends to be particularly harsh and destructive. As the force of antagonism increases in each film, the threat of death becomes more imminent. By definition, Brasco is highly vulnerable, constantly reminded how crossing his mob associates could have fatal results. Lefty, his main supporter, is responsible for twenty-six hits. The head of their family is assassinated in an ongoing internal power struggle that soon involves Brasco directly. After Lefty and their immediate superior, Sonny Black, ambush and slaughter the head of their territory, Sonny Red, Donnie is brought to the scene, sure, because they've "called" for him, that he, too, will die. Instead he is enlisted to help cut up and dispose of the bodies. An ill-conceived FBI plan to use Brasco to set up a gambling operation in Florida inadvertently exposes him to discovery and elimination. One of the mob nearly sees him leaving a meeting with his FBI controllers. Later, a photo of a yacht the bureau gives Brasco to use appears in a national news magazine, revealed as part of the

ABSCAM operation. It is as though the organization he works for acts as his own worst enemy (see fig. 21).

Althea Flynt's efforts to be a true partner to her husband eventually separate them. While the judicial system beleaguers Larry Flynt, Althea's condition brought on by drug use worsens, and she contracts AIDS. She progressively deteriorates. It becomes difficult for her to talk, to move without being assisted, and her appearance becomes ghastly. She loses weight, her face becomes increasingly pale, circles grow and darken under her eyes, while she dyes her hair in various fluorescent shades. As in *Brasco,* death draws near when conflict evolves toward climax. While the Supreme Court is hearing Flynt's arguments, Althea accidentally drowns in the bathtub, too weak to prevent herself from sinking below the surface of the water.

Helfgott's preparations to perform the Rachmaninoff piano concerto for his college recital absorb him and progressively isolate him from contact with normal, everyday life. He neglects his appearance. He goes down to the foyer of his apartment building to get his mail unaware that he is naked from the waist down. Critic Terrance Rafferty comments that "the idea that creativity is *dangerous*—that the true artist is always playing with fire, risking emotional self-immolation—is immensely comforting both to filmmakers, for whom the notion functions as a self-aggrandizing heroic myth, and to the audience, for whom it provides a there-but-for-the-grace-of-God cautionary moral" (116). Helfgott's performance of the concerto brings the film to a preliminary climax, suggesting that the fire of his drive has burned too brightly, and that by attaining this goal, Helfgott has burned himself out. The sound of the concert, the scene's ostensible reason for being, fades out, and instead the emphasis becomes the extra-close-up, slow motion shots of the huge drops of sweat being flung from David's face and hair, suggesting that his very essence has been wrung out and flung upon the keys and floorboards of the stage. Helfgott receives his ovation, "then promptly pays the price for the exhilarating release of all the tension and guilt and competitive desire that have been building up in him; he collapses onstage, sodden with sweat, as if the effort to resolve his barely understood experience had wholly depleted his resources" (118).

Trials. With this initial climax, the film marks the end of the period of David Helfgott's life when he is victimized by the destructive influence of patriarchal systems. The development of his ability so that he could give this concert has created one kind of trial for him; his subsequent efforts to redefine himself and eventually return to performance function as a second set of trials from which he eventually emerges triumphant. In the second half of the film, rather than working under the constraints of patriarchal influences of father and teacher, he is supported primarily by two women. Sylvia owns Moby's and becomes his friend and employer. Gillian, Sylvia's friend, becomes his wife and personal manager. In a final moment of trial, in the midst of the momentum of his new life, Peter appears in the doorway of David's room. He attempts to reinstate something of his former relationship with his son by once more inviting David to tell with him the story about the broken violin. Now David refuses to provide the punch line and tells his father to leave. This final banishing of the old validates the verdict David's new life has placed on it.

Brasco and *Flynt* also provide evidence to support the idea that docudramas favor depicting the development of conflict in terms of literal and/or figurative trials. Part of the irony of Joe Pistone's dilemma is that the closer emotionally he becomes to Lefty in the role of Donnie Brasco, the more damage he can do in his original role as undercover officer. In becoming indispensable to Lefty, Donnie faces a series of figurative tests and trials, such as the discovery of the tape recorder hidden in his boot when the "boys" go to a Japanese teahouse and must remove their shoes, or the tests of his loyalty when he must help dispose of the bodies of Sonny Red and his crew. These culminate when Brasco, with Lefty's help, is to "make his bones" by murdering Sonny Red's former right-hand man. He is forced to play his role to its extreme, logical conclusion, by going to the brink of pulling the trigger. A last-second bust saves him from crossing the line and becoming his role completely. These simultaneous trials of his loyalty to both masters are reminders of the actual legal process that eventually attains the hundreds of convictions Donnie's evidence makes possible.

Larry Flynt's story argues that his work as a publisher leads him to become a full-time proponent of the First Amendment and critic of the judicial system. The stakes in Flynt's court battles increase from a local to national, federal scale, eventually pitting him against Jerry Falwell in an appeal to the U.S. Supreme Court. He spends less time at work and more time in court, or in jail because of contempt charges for inappropriate courtroom behavior. Parallel to his partnership with Althea is his volatile friendship with Alan, his lawyer, who must work as much to control his client as to be his advocate. The series of formal trials Flynt faces, much like Brasco's juggling of his conflicting roles, and Helfgott's need to perform at the piano, suggest that literal and figurative trials confirm the main characters' abilities to work and argue that the work itself is necessary and valuable despite its costs.

Articulation. True to their melodramatic telling of true stories, these docudramas move toward narrative closure that articulates and clarifies moral values. *Brasco, Flynt,* and *Shine* conclude their stories in scenes that show the balance of achievement and cost. In a brief ceremony, Joe Pistone receives a citation and a check for $500 rewarding him for his accomplishments under cover. Larry Flynt receives the news about his victory in the Supreme Court by telephone. David Helfgott receives ovations when once more he performs before enthusiastic concert audiences. The reward for each man's survival is moral victory. Pistone is recognized by the peers who have dealt with him skeptically throughout. Flynt's work is recognized as deserving of First Amendment protection. Helfgott emerges from his breakdown a good enough man to be both husband and artist. In each case, however, the clearest articulation of the cost of what work has accomplished is the emphatic treatment of absence.

Just before Pistone's citation ceremony, Lefty receives a phone call, then dons his jacket to leave his apartment. We have been led to expect that Donnie's treachery has resulted in a summons for Lefty to be accountable. Lefty pauses before he leaves; in close-up he slips his watch from his wrist and puts it and the rest of his jewelry in a drawer where his wife will find it. The camera lingers on the dresser drawer as Lefty exits the frame. His valuables are, in essence, his remains, poor compensation for his removal from his role as husband, provider, and friend. Similarly, in the next scene, when Joe is handed his bonus for the years of endangering his life and his marriage, his wife is at his side, suggesting the marriage may have survived—but at what cost? In these final moments, the film computes the price of justice in human currency.

Flynt also weighs accomplishment in terms of loss. In a scene in the vast master bedroom, just before Flynt gets the news of his penultimate court victory, we hear Althea talking to him. For a moment, it is unclear whether the sound of the dead woman's voice is a memory or perhaps an hallucination. The camera tracks through the empty room, following the sound of the voice, to find Flynt laying on the bed, absorbed in an old videotape of a young and healthy Althea playing seductively before the camera. The phone rings; Alan tells him he's won. After they hang up, Flynt continues to talk to her moving image, urging her to "strip for me," using photographic presence to deter, at least momentarily, the fact of her physical absence. "I'll never be old and ugly," her voice continues, "I'm going to live forever." Both Flynts have been able to get what they want.

In *Shine,* Peter Helfgott's final appearance, brief attempt at reconciliation, and subsequent banishment are a reminder of what the relationship has cost both father and son. At first Peter's bulk fills the doorway of David's small room above the wine bar, where he has just finished another enthusiastically received set. David looks up, sees Peter standing there, and drops the dish he has been holding. He tries to continue what he'd started by opening up a can, but his hands are shaking too much. Peter takes the can and opener from him. "Let me show you how easy it is," Peter says. "No one will love you like me." David will not look at his father and, by short circuiting the old story of the violin, refuses to resume their relationship; when he can finally look up again, the space his father had filled is empty once more, for good. The film concludes with David and Gillian putting flowers on Peter's grave.

As in *Brasco* and *Flynt,* the cinematic figuring of absence here expresses the price of survival. Survival has been each person's triumph over his victimization and proves why each one is exemplary. Each man's work creates the risk but also provides the means to survive. Each survival story testifies to finding the resources necessary to attain goals in spite of the antagonism of law and patriarchy. Ironically, these two ideological systems that one expects would support the struggle of men to attain their desires act repressively in these stories instead. Law does not help a law enforcement officer; a publisher is harmed as much as helped in his efforts to exercise his First Amendment rights; a son becomes an artist and complete person in spite of his father's efforts simultaneously to create and contain his accomplishments. Each example argues that survival itself can be an important victory over destructively constraining ideologies and, consequently, that the accomplishment of survival is an important form of empowerment.

Ghosts of Mississippi, Rosewood, Amistad

As they tell their separate stories of men and their work, *Brasco, Flynt,* and *Shine* become male melodramas, case studies of the effects of patriarchy, rooted in the real. Much in the same way that these films show us the contradictory and self-destructive tendencies of values, prejudices, and behaviors rooted in a patriarchal ideology, recent features addressing issues of race center on the deliberate ignorance of injustice by the justice system itself. The feature film presentations of historical material in *Ghosts of Mississippi, Rosewood,* and *Amistad* also share the same basic structure that was evident in *Brasco, Flynt,* and *Shine.* The idea systems revolving around matters of race and justice act antagonistically toward the victims whose stories we are watching. In two of the three films, victims have the opportunity to gain justice through formal trials. In the third case, the very point of the *Rosewood* story is that no formal trial ever occurred. Here victims and victimizers are "tried" informally. As all three of these films bring their stories to a close, their emphasis of absent people and places provides moral clarification of the issues the stories articulate.

Victims. In their very different stories of racial injustice *Ghosts, Rosewood,* and *Amistad* each show the legal system itself as a cause of victimization. Victims are hurt by harms the system tolerates. The films argue that a system of laws that ignores or even supports harms committed because of race violates its own purpose and acts self-destructively, if its racism is left uncorrected. The *Amistad* story occurs at a point in history when American law tolerated slavery. *Rosewood* shows the results of the law looking aside and allowing a town to seek "justice" as a lynch mob. The courts in *Ghosts* attempt to avoid bringing a politically volatile case to trial. *Amistad* and *Ghosts* argue that the legal system is capable of self-correction; the transgressions of courts that attempt to operate selectively will come to light eventually. The unwillingness and inability of law to operate in *Rosewood* leads quickly to anarchy and annihilation.

The "work" of the male main characters of each of these films begins with the damage that is done when they and others are denied the due process of law. Each film shows victims being created by the sudden, brutal shattering of the order of their lives. The legal systems that might offer justice in their cases only exacerbate the wrongs done to each victim. Medgar Evers is shot in the back while he is getting out of his car after coming home from work. Cinque's story in *Amistad* begins when he is waylaid, captured, and thrown into slavery. Just as Mr. Mann rides into Rosewood and decides to settle there, wholesale, irrational violence erupts against the community he has decided to join.

The inadequacies of justice extend the initial damage done by violence. No representatives of law come forward to help the people of Rosewood. After Cinque and his group of fellow slaves-turned-mutineers are victimized by the slave system that captures them, they escape, only to find themselves at the mercy of a system of laws ill suited to determine their fate. They are thrust into a legal quagmire when the *Amistad* is captured off Connecticut shores. The group remains imprisoned for years because questions of their rights as human beings are secondary to conflicting issues of jurisdiction, obligations under international treaties, the status of those born into slavery as opposed to those sold into it, and rights of salvage of the vessel and its cargo. Medgar Evers's widow Myrlie must wait through three decades and as many trials in order for her husband's case to receive a fair hearing. The Everses' story becomes the story of the victimization of Bobby DeLaughter, the district attorney who finally takes up their cause. DeLaughter's prosecution of a popular white supremacist poisons his career politically. His wife leaves him. His family is subjected to death threats.

The strong possibility of death hangs over all of these stories. The threat of death that punctuates *Ghosts* is even more imminent in *Rosewood*, where the lynch mob is clearly taking no prisoners, and in *Amistad*, as the Africans face equally likely guilty verdicts: guilty of murder, or guilty of being property that must be returned to the slavers who claim to own them.

All three films give systems that promote racism an explicitly self-destructive edge. Slavery in *Amistad* appears determined to ruin its own product if not destroy it. Only the strong survive the conditions in the slave ship holds. During the Middle Passage sequence, the slavers throw dozens of slaves overboard, chained to weighted rocks, to avoid having to feed them. Justice derails itself when the Mississippi legal system appears to resist determining who killed Medgar Evers. While Myrlie Evers is testifying during one of the first trials of Byron De La Beckwith, the governor of Mississippi walks in and shakes the defendant's hand. Myrlie Evers mentions the moment repeatedly, suggesting that the blatant display of favoritism, rather than discourage her, has helped motivate her to pursue the case for thirty years. To make the point that the lynch mob in *Rosewood* is destroying its own interests, the first victim it murders is "Aunt" Sarah Carrier, the community midwife. Aunt Sarah is shot in the stomach while she stands on the front porch of her house, confronting a mob of men who all knew her as the person who had helped their own mothers and wives bring children into the world.

Individual survival in each film becomes a matter of the epic endurance required to navigate upstream against the current of opposing systems. Myrlie Evers describes her thirty-year search for justice as "a very personal mission, researching, inquiring, praying that something, any hint of evidence would be found to reaffirm the case. . . . I was prepared to keep my promise to Medgar to go with him the last mile of the way" ("Ghosts of Mississippi," *Jet* 30 Dec. 1996–6 Jan. 1997: 61). *Amistad* and *Rosewood* are both holocaust stories, depicting incidents from which genocide erupts. Just as the white mob seeks to obliterate the property and residents of Rosewood, to erase completely the existence of the community, so too would the international slave trade appropriate the lives of Cinque and the rest of the *Amistad* Africans though subjugation. Under these conditions, survival is success. Mr. Mann's ability to overcome the bullets, fires, and ropes of Rosewood is comparable to Cinque's struggles within the confines of slave ships and courtrooms. The films argue that simply to emerge intact from the constraints of these systems is a major victory.

Trials. Literal or figurative trials in these films define the terms of survival. *Ghosts* and *Amistad* set out survival courses for their main characters that cover the hard ground of no less than three trials in each film. When both films turn to courtroom drama, the legal process itself is as much on trial as the litigants. Bobby DeLaughter takes up Myrlie Evers's cause only to encounter strong resistance to trying the case thirty years after De La Beckwith's second mistrial. Few witnesses remain alive, evidence has disappeared; incredibly, even the trial transcripts are missing. He finds the crucial piece of evidence, De La Beckwith's rifle, tucked away in a trunk in the study of his own former father-in-law, a respected judge. Similarly, through the successive trials of the *Amistad* Africans, the key issues shift from their actions to the laws that define their status: Are they slaves and therefore property, or are they human beings with rights to free themselves from bondage? As both stories turn attention to the workings of justice, the legal representatives of the central characters become the main characters. This happens early on in *Ghosts;* after opening scenes sketch the events of the 1960s, the story proper begins in Bobby DeLaughter's office, just before Myrlie Evers walks in to ask for help. Much as the narrative focus in this film shifts from the African American widow to her white male lawyer, *Amistad* also, as it moves from crisis to climax, becomes the story of Cinque's lawyer, John Quincy Adams.

Rosewood also uses agency in order to show what is necessary for the people in its story to endure trials in order to survive. In this case, however, it is a fictional black character who represents the interests of the story's African American victims, a variation on docudramatic form I will discuss below at greater length. Despite creating a fictional main character, it remains that of these three films, *Rosewood* is the least susceptible to the problem of appropriation, whereas asking whose story is receiving dramatic attention in *Ghosts* and *Amistad* points us toward how the docudramatic versions of the stories of Myrlie Evers and Cinque become the stories of their agents.

Articulation. The literal and figurative trials the characters endure in these films articulate the costs of survival and empowerment. Trials exist in part to allow opportunities for articulation. In each story, trials illuminate the consequences of racism and its accompanying intolerance and hatred. Beyond what can be expressed within and because of the trial forum, however, the outcomes in both *Ghosts* and *Amistad* show the legal system possessing not only constraints but also the possibility of self-rectification.

One lesson *Ghosts* provides is that it takes patience and perseverance, but the system can still correct itself. Similarly, the *Amistad* story illustrates how the system of appeals to progressively higher courts, along with its potential for abuse through political prosecutions, necessarily maintains its capacity to assess itself.

As was true in *Brasco, Flynt,* and *Shine,* it is the figuring of absence in *Ghosts, Rosewood,* and *Amistad* that provides the most powerful moments of articulation. At the conclusion of *Ghosts,* Myrlie Evers stands after the verdict has been brought against De La Beckwith and speaks directly to the spirit of Medgar Evers, telling him of their victory. *Amistad* ends with the image of Cinque standing on the prow of a ship returning him to Africa, while subtitles inform us that his village was no longer there, and that his wife and the children he had wished to return to through the years of his incarceration and trial were also gone, in all likelihood, taken into slavery. *Rosewood* begins with an aerial tracking shot following a red, dusty road running past a small collection of houses, barns, and shops. The same shot that bookends the conclusion of the film shows the leveled, smoking rubble; only the outlines of the foundations remain where every structure of the town once stood (see figs. 22 and 23).

Instructive Positions

The basic purpose of docudramatic articulation is to clarify moral issues at stake in the world a film depicts. At the same time, a docudrama warrants its persuasive argument by showing how it has anchored its presentation in actuality, in the material of the real. Selecting a "true" story to be told frames the outline of a film's moral system; subsequent narrative structures must address the questions raised logically by offering this argument by example. We are positioned initially to ask, Why choose this particular story to tell? Why and how is this story exemplary? What do we learn because this is a true story? Articulation arises, then, as a result of strategies of exemplification. The opportunity to view the respective stories of Joe Pistone, Larry Flynt, David Helfgott, Bobby DeLaughter, Cinque, and the people of Rosewood through the prism of docudrama shows us how their survival becomes exemplary. If their survival singles out these people, suggesting that their experiences are worthy of story, a second strategy of exemplification results from showing them specifically as survivors of trials. The spectacle of a trial further separates participants from observers, distinguishing between the watchers and the watched. Not surprisingly, in all of these films, as central characters undergo literal and figurative trials, their communities are present as spectators, often as juries. When communities appear in these films as audiences, their spectatorship instructs our own. Central, exemplary figures tend to find themselves in the position of needing vindication from their communities. Consequently, the process of their vindication focuses the moral issues at stake in the world of a film. Depicting a surviving individual as exemplary, showing exemplary individuals in relationship to their community, and displaying community as audience positions us to perceive as instructive the witnessing and validation of survival. These strategies warrant the films' arguments by example.

Throughout *Shine,* for example, David's artistry as a pianist is only part of what separates him from everyone else; once he is on the road to recovery, each performance becomes a trial, an opportunity to show that he can "make it" through the music and emerge intact. The enthusiastic reception of his performances by increasingly larger audiences (first at Moby's, then the concert hall) affirms the success of his "cure." Larry Flynt separates himself from the norm in equally extraordinary ways. In order to dramatize the hypocrisy and injustice of prosecuting him for exercising his constitutional rights, Flynt begins to appear at his trials wearing an army helmet and a diaper made of the American flag. He is vindicated in court almost despite his desire to call attention to his cause. Donnie Brasco is forced to perform extraordinarily on occasion in order to ensure that his audience, his peers in the mob, will continue to perceive him as ordinary, as one of them. When the wire he wears in his boot will be revealed because patrons at a Japanese teahouse are asked to remove their shoes, he finds himself forced to create a distraction by beating the managers of the establishment. He proves himself again to his on-screen audience, his community of peers, later when he helps them cut up the bodies of Sonny Red and his associates. At the film's close, he receives a citation before his other peers, the FBI agents he works with. Cinque in *Amistad,* as the leader of the mutiny, becomes the spokesperson for the group of Africans both in and outside of the trials they face.

Exemplification in each case necessitates a dual action. The exemplary attributes and accomplishments of the main character distance him from his community; consequently, he must strengthen his sense of connection to important groups. Helfgott thrives because of the contact with his supportive audiences. Flynt needs the group that helped him start *Hustler* in order to continue to publish the magazine. They in turn weather his extremes of erratic behavior. Ironically, it is the very "contemporary community standards" his opponents would use in court to suppress his work that Flynt argues he is serving. Bobby DeLaughter must emerge from the small town politics of his own office and the community he serves in order to bring Myrlie Evers's cause to trial; however, it is that same community he must convince at trial in order to win a just verdict.

Throughout these films, communities appear during scenes of judgment and vindication as audiences *(Shine, Brasco, Flynt, Rosewood)*, often specifically as spectators and the juries in courtrooms *(Flynt, Ghosts, Amistad)*. These recurring audience/performance configurations suture us into the scene as vicarious participants, positioned to benefit from the instructive value of witnessing both exemplary performance and the response it receives from its filmic audience.

One element that tends to distinguish feature film from television docudrama is that while MOWs also develop iconographies of audience, particularly favoring courtroom scenes with juries and spectators, the groups in the features function more as characters. MOWs emphasize interaction of their principal characters, while community/jury/spectator configurations provide backdrop. Features, shaping narrative to their larger screens, gravitate toward spectacle, so that groups are involved directly in character actions, or entire groups act as characters. For example, in *Shine,* Helfgott's sisters witness their father's abuse of David; near the end of the film, in David's concluding, triumphant concert, they, as well as Rosen, his old teacher, appear within the audience as it rises in ovation to the performance. This audience, much like the "first" audiences he encounters at Moby's, confirm his identity, his sense of self as artist. Recurring scenes of the group of fellow magazine managers in *Flynt* trace the development of the publisher's legal dilemmas. The uniformity of their individual responses at any time creates a tendency for the group to act as a single entity that reflects on the value of his cause, as do the recurring reactions of the group of *Amistad* Africans Cinque must speak and act for.

Rosewood

Of all these films, *Rosewood* develops to the greatest extent an iconography of groups acting as characters. In contrast to the five other feature film docudramas released in 1997, *Rosewood* is not any one person's "true story" but, instead, uses as its point of historical reference a white community's successful efforts to annihilate its African American neighbor. *Rosewood*'s opening and closing sequences address a question fundamental to filmic representation of the real: How can a work show the fact that something that was there no longer exists? The sequences dramatize the absence, the inaccessibility of subject, that is the very premise for docudramatization. The impetus for telling the *Rosewood* story as film docudrama is that unlike

Amistad, the story of the town of Rosewood truly was a "quieted" chapter of African American history.[4] Survivors were induced more than sixty years after the events to testify before the Florida legislature, providing a context for the resulting docudrama narrative. *Rosewood,* in essence, is the story of a group of witnesses that survived not only the holocaust of the lynch mob that destroyed their town and families but also subsequent threats never to tell anyone about it (Dye 28). In shaping this story as docudrama, Singleton's film adapts its original texts, the newspaper accounts, and survivor testimonies that were emerging decades after the fact, by placing communities in the positions of antagonist and protagonist, with individuals emerging as exemplars from each group to represent and articulate group desires. At moments of confrontation, the film shows events from the viewpoints of witnesses who are invariably the children who will later become the sources of the story we are watching.

The film allocates the survival of confrontation to both black and white witnesses. The lynch mob first assaults its victims when it disrupts a Carrier family dinner celebrating the birthday of one of Sylvester Carrier's children. When the mob claims its first victim, Aunt Sarah, the children of the Carrier family are huddled inside the house, watching her failed attempt to turn back the mob. They also believe, as we do, that Sylvester is shot trying to defend his home. In a parallel configuration, one of the more vicious, bloodthirsty, trigger-happy members of the white mob, Duke Purdy, repeatedly brings his own preadolescent son along so that the lynchings can give the boy lessons in how to be a man, lessons the boy eventually rejects.

Just as Sylvester exemplifies the Rosewood community's futile efforts at self-defense, Purdy becomes the most extreme example of the racism of the people of Sumner. Caught between the two communities is John Wright, the white storekeeper who serves both black and white customers. The film faithfully re-creates the actual Wright's ultimate commitment to helping the victims by sheltering a group of black children in his own home, running devastating risks from which he would otherwise have been exempt. The film also portrays Wright's role in aiding in the rescue of surviving women and children by train. Just as depicting witnesses as children instructs us as to the nature of the heritage of the Rosewood story, so too does the shaping of the actual John Wright into a feature film character. We first see Wright having sex in the back of his store with one of the teenage Carrier girls who clerks for him. By the end of the film, he has developed from hypocritical racist exploiter to a man who can act on the basis of some sense of decency, so that as the most prominent white character, his changes provide an argument by example to the film's white audience.

Rosewood, unlike other films in the group, creates a fictional main character, Mr. Mann, as a further means to shape its documentary material to fit into feature film conventions. Several critics have faulted *Rosewood* for its conventionality in depicting Mr. Mann as "the mysterious stranger of a thousand westerns" (Schickel 83), who is "a loner, home from the war, looking to settle down to a peaceful life if only his new neighbors didn't desperately need his help. But they do" (Maslin, "Black Man" C18). Mann appears in the film riding a horse, wearing a ten-gallon hat, a duster, and, because he is a veteran of the World War, carrying twin .45 automatics in crossed bandoliers, rather than two holstered six-shooters. A succession of his scenes demand Western-like action: He must save himself in a shoot-out with a pursuing lynch mob; extricate himself from a hangman's noose when the mob does catch him; and help the save the surviving women and children of the town by rescuing them with a moving train.

E. R. Shipp argues that rather than simply recycling Western genre conventions, *Rosewood,* like other recent works by African American filmmakers, instead is constructing an "alternative to conventional popular culture narratives" for its audience (26). Shipp's observation suggests that rather than allowing a story about African American history to become a story about white male characters, instead, in this instance, the story's docudramatic narrative structure has translated for its own purposes the visual vocabulary of the Western genre. In arguing for the terms of survival, *Rosewood* appropriates its own narrative material. The film's efforts to construct an "alternative" narrative create, in effect, an alternative mythology. In becoming a story about survival and empowerment, *Rosewood* attempts to empower itself, and the audience it addresses.[5]

The iconography of the Western *Rosewood* incorporates by showing Mann as the outsider—who rides in, would settle on a small spread in the community, survives the hangman's noose, and defends himself and the surviving women and children of the community with his guns—sets up cues that instruct our reading of the film. To frame the story as a Western not only provides the possibility of an alternative mythology but also allows for a critical reading of the cultural values the ideology of Westerns customarily conveys. The film points toward a redefinition and an appropriation for a black audience of basic Western film elements such as community and heroism. Even more, if, in the Western, the mythic frontier is typically a site of convergence of structural contradictions (nature vs. culture; old vs. new; east vs. west; etc.), it prompts seeking a comparable set of antinomies in the *Rosewood* narrative, such as black (civilization) vs. white (savagery); nurture vs. annihilation; creation vs. destruction; exposure vs. repression; and honesty vs. hypocrisy. *Rosewood*'s adaptation of the Western film structure suggests that a racial "frontier" exists in American social history that necessitates a mythology of presentation. The traditional conventions of the Western become auto-critical in this reassignment. More basically, it suggests that an audience fluent in the vocabulary of the traditional film Western, potentially can read the resituation of Western conventions as they are applied here. The docudramatic construction of *Rosewood* foregrounds both its source texts, the "true story" historical material it re-creates, and the generic conventions the film adapts in its shaping of its historical sources.

Rosewood's foregrounding of its conventions is just as instructive as its configuring of community as audience, with surviving witnesses underlining the historical importance of the events we see them see. By doing so, the film is highlighting the materials and methods of its construction, creating a kind of "signposting" of its sources comparable to other kinds of indications (intertitles; on-screen presentation of sources) that demonstrate the confluence of texts producing docudramatic argument. As the film promotes an awareness of its materials and methods, it reminds us of the constructedness of the view of history it presents even as it re-views, resituates, and offers a critical reading of the traditional values we have come to understand to be embedded within the contradictions that traditionally have conveyed such views.

How Spielberg Added *Amistad* to His *List*

The fate of the *Amistad* story consistently has been that it foregrounds its importance as narrative and its relationship with its audience. More than forty years before the release of Steven Spielberg's feature film, William A. Owens began his account of the events by noting that the *Amistad* was brought to harbor in the United States with a preestablished, sensationalized reputation. Newspaper stories publicized sightings of the mysterious "ghost ship" for weeks before it was captured and contained much speculation about the black pirates and cannibals who apparently occupied it (3–4). Exploitation as entertainment of the *Amistad* Africans continued to feed the opinion climate surrounding their capture, years of imprisonment, and progress through the American judicial system. The long-running play *The Black Schooner, or the Pirate Slaver Amistad* opened within one week of the ship's seizure by the American navy. While imprisoned in Connecticut, the group of captives received each day as many as five thousand visitors, who paid the jailer (who commissioned a wax museum exhibit and a 135-foot panoramic mural of the battle to take over the ship) an admission fee of twelve and a half cents each (Jackson 117–18). After the U.S. Supreme Court decision "immediately" freed the *Amistad* Africans, Cinque and nine of the group were taken by their sponsors on a seven-month fund-raising tour that helped finance their return and the establishment of the mission that accompanied them. In their program appearances, they would tell their story and demonstrate the extent of their conversion to Christianity (Cable 119–20).

In the months before the release of the film, producer Debbie Allen stated in a number of interviews that she was drawn to the story originally because she had not been taught this chapter of African American history at Howard University, that it was a "lost," "quieted" story that would highlight issues about the teaching and writing of history ("Amistad," *Jet* 22 Dec. 1997: 60–61). Consequently, she optioned the Owens book in the early-1980s and spent years attempting to interest a filmmaker before the success of *Schindler's List* drew her together with Spielberg. That the story was "lost" would have come as a surprise not only to Owens, whose book was first published in 1953 and reprinted in 1968, but also to Mary Cable, who told the story as *Black Odyssey: The Case of the Slave Ship Amistad* (1971), and to Howard Jones, whose *Mutiny on the Amistad* (1987) appeared two years before Barbara Chase-Riboud's version of the story was published as *Echo of Lions* (1989). Clearly, the issue is not a matter of whether or not the story has been "there" as much as what has been done to make an audience aware of its presence.

Certainly, in late-1997, *Amistad* would find an audience ready for a film that told about enslaved Africans finding justice in the American system. In the months surrounding the release of the film, the U. S. Congress and the American press launched a prominent discussion of the question of the need for a national apology for slavery (Alter 62). The stage had been set by the recent publication of a group of books that reevaluated slavery as an historical institution.[6] Throughout the year, several other theatrical films targeting an African American audience were released or were in production, beginning with John Singleton's *Rosewood,* including also *Soul Food* (K. Edmonds 1997); *Eve's Bayou* (K. Lemmons and S. Jackson 1997); and *Beloved* (J. Demme and O. Winfrey 1998) (Farley 86–87). The name "Amistad" itself became something of a cultural icon, with the production of a national opera coinciding with the release of the film, the publication of seven related books (including a children's version of the story), the 1997 publication of a new narrative of the mutiny (by David Pesci), and the broadcasting on cable of two documentaries "timed to ride the coattails" of the feature release, including *Ship of Slaves* (History Channel) and the biography *Cinque* (Arts and Entertainment) (James 8).

Spielberg's *Amistad* attempts to appeal persuasively to its audience precisely as a story about storytelling. The feature film adaptation addresses the problem of slavery in contemporary terms. Specifically, the Spielberg adaptation equates storytelling with empowerment and intercultural collaboration. As the *Amistad* story becomes structured by the progress of its main characters through the American legal system, the film (in contrast to print versions of the story) uses docudrama form to argue that storytelling can right the wrongs perpetuated against victims. Institutions here create victims by denying them opportunities to speak. The film depicts empowerment as the progressive opportunity to articulate how injustice has been done. Articulation in the film clarifies the experience of injustice. More importantly, however, the fact of articulation signifies the refusal to be enslaved, the first step toward empowerment. As a docudrama, the film ultimately clarifies the value of articulation. It argues further that articulation in this case is limited by necessary translation, representation, and reception by its audience.

Spielberg's *Amistad* distinguishes itself from print versions of the story by the rigor of its emphasis on articulation. There is a core pattern of development common to the group of *Amistad* narratives. The basic story consists of a series of parallel movements. Shifts that are geographical (the travel of the *Amistad* group from Africa to Cuba to the United States) entail sociopolitical changes (from life in Africa to captivity in slavery to captivity within the American judicial system).

Within the larger cultural and political oppositions that provide a common structure to all versions of the story (Africa vs. America; black vs. white; captivity vs. freedom; property vs. person; institution vs. individual), Spielberg gives his story a melodramatic focus by foregrounding the process of articulation. The narrative movements serve to emphasize why the need to tell a story arises, the process by which the story is formed, finds its audience, and is heard, allowing the story to reach completion. As melodrama, Spielberg's film shows articulation arising as a necessary response to victimization. The institutional experiences of the African characters show the changing nature of their vulnerability as they face repressive social systems, first exploitation under slavery, then processing through the American courts that threaten to return them to the slave system they have perhaps only temporarily eluded. Avoiding danger ultimately depends upon their ability to make their case. Articulation, the film argues, is the means to empowerment.

"Articulation" here means expression that is both meaningful and effective. Articulation entails having the capability and opportunity to speak to a responsive audience. Empowerment, acquiring the means (the "power") to attain a desired goal (in this case, freedom) occurs for the *Amistad* Africans through progressive stages of articulation. Beginning from a relatively powerless state of linguistic alienation, they gradually gain capability. They encounter a receptive audience and acquire both language and agents to express their position with increasing effectiveness.

The film begins by defining the *Amistad* prisoners visually and aurally in terms of difference and separation. They are chained in the hold and only partially clothed. The white men sailing the ship are conventionally Western by comparison. The most important barrier, we soon see, becomes language. The violent action of the mutiny that opens the film reverses the roles of captor and captive only temporarily. The successful mutiny— the loosening of bonds, the ability to overpower and kill white men armed with guns—presents limited freedom and power. What the prisoners really want is the power to return home to the lives and freedom taken from them when they were enslaved. The newly unchained men brandish machetes and argue freely among themselves. We, along with the Spanish-speaking men they now hold prisoner, are excluded from understanding the words they exchange; however, when their leader (Cinque) drags one of the Spaniards over to the ship's steering wheel and points with his blade at the rising sun, the intentions are clear—sail the ship back where it came from. Cinque suspects deception and tries to steer the ship himself. Eventually, they end up not in Africa but off the coast of the United States. The Africans have traded the physical victimization of slavery (chains; whips; drowning; starvation) for cultural victimization. The film conveys to us their sense of alienation in part by showing the frustration of having the daunting task of making others, who don't speak their language, make the ship work and also by having the entirety of the dialogue in this sequence remain untranslated and unsubtitled. Without common language, cultural difference is mutually exclusive.

When they are captured by the American navy, the Africans pass from captivity in one institution, slavery, to detention in another, the American judicial system. They are still held captive behind bars; however, the nature of the constraints change. Slavery as an institution requires that the line between master and slave never be crossed. Its existence enforces the slave's complete subjugation of self. Linguistic disregard is elemental to dehumanization under slavery. We see in one scene that the men arbitrarily have been given Spanish names that they cannot respond to since the sounds are meaningless to them.

The legal system, on the other hand, while still repressive, demands articulation. Self-defense allows the opportunity for self-presentation. Self-explanation becomes a particularly critical issue for this group of defendants, since they must prove in a court of law that they are human beings, rather than property. Their passage from exclusion to inclusion (within the "rules" of civilization) begins when the defense team, in order to do its job, attempts to determine where the prisoners came from and, therefore, what language it is they speak. In a sequence that enacts the beginning of the movement from cultural separation to commonality, a linguistic consultant determines the words the prisoners speak for elemental numbers, goes to the waterfront, and, by counting from one to ten repeatedly, eventually finds someone who responds in kind, by picking up the count with him. The young sailor, James Covey, becomes the translator for the defense. The small group of abolitionists and lawyers creates the first sympathetic audience the Africans encounter.

In this spirit, the defense early on solicits the help of John Quincy Adams in dealing with the case's conflation of legal and political issues. He declines to become involved, but to help the lawyers help the Africans, he asks, "What is their story?" Whoever can tell the best story in a court of law, Adams suggests, will win.

As the film depicts the progress of the Africans toward empowerment through the process of becoming capable of articulating their case to listeners, their lawyers (and eventually Adams) and Covey become their agents. Agency (in the form of language and speaker capable of representation) mediates between individual and institution. One scene graphically shows how cultural difference necessitates agency, and how agency is integral to articulation. To prove that the group came originally from Africa, rather than Cuba, Cinque testifies about the Middle Passage, the voyage across the Atlantic from Sierra Leone to Havana. Covey translates while Cinque speaks, joining in English the pace and cadence of Cinque's words in their native Mende (see fig. 24). The words become largely replaced by the scenes they narrate, showing first brief images of Cinque's life in Africa, before he is overpowered and dragged into captivity; the cliffside fortress at Lomboko, where thousands are stored before they are shipped to the slave market in Cuba; the conditions in the hold of the slaver that crosses the Atlantic; the treatment of their human cargo by their captors. The verbal narration drops out as we see dozens of men, women, and children being dragged overboard to the ocean bottom, locked into chains weighted by rocks. The testimony, shown like the images of a recuperated nightmare, positions subjective experience simultaneously within multiple institutional frames: language, the experience of slavery, and the trial procedure itself. As one critic noted, after "we go beneath history's surface where terrible truth floats down to us—lost knowledge, history's secrets no longer forgotten," the cut back to the courtroom makes the spectators there, as well as the film's viewers, witnesses to what would be otherwise repressed (A. White 40). Covey's translation makes the experience of these victims accessible. Their testimony marks their passage from victims to witnesses. They now can affect the workings of the institution. Articulation furthers the process of empowerment.

The film shows storytelling as a counterforce, a necessary response to the ways that victimized individuals are at the mercy of repressive institutions. For their story to function fully, to bring justice out of injustice, it must be told before successive audiences in a series of trials. Appropriately enough, it is Adams himself who must become a final agent for the Africans, completing their story before their ulterior audience in the film, the U.S. Supreme Court.

The film's narrative chain positions Adams as the final, necessary link in allowing the storytelling process to reach completion. He tries to maintain a distance from the trial. Baldwin sends a written appeal to Adams for assistance when presidential interference threatens to deny the Africans the justice that they have won in the U.S. District Court. Adams still hesitates to become involved.

The film suggests that Adams's moment of commitment occurs when he meets Cinque and they discuss together the circumstances the case is facing. The scene offers cinematic equivalents of equality, a meeting of the minds (see fig. 25). The two men walk together through Adams's hothouse, sharing jointly the space of the scene. They pause before a potted African violet that Cinque touches with the same delicacy we have seen in Adams while he cares for his plants. Cinque (through Covey) tells Adams that he knows he will emerge victorious because he will call upon his ancestors, and they will help him through the trial he faces. Subsequently, it is Cinque's words that Adams paraphrases as he summarizes the defense's case before the Supreme Court. His relationship with Cinque is a collaboration, providing him, the scene suggests, with the enlightenment he needs to articulate the case effectively.

The summation scene not only draws together the film's equation of articulation and empowerment but also shows how articulation throughout the film has been directed at moral clarification. Adams uses Cinque's ancestral values to argue, in essence, that like people, the court and the country need to be the best of what has brought them into existence. In the blocking of the scene, he moves to stand before a row of busts of the Founding Fathers, one of whom is his own father, John Adams. "Who we are," he says, "is who we *were*" (see fig. 26).

The successive scenes showing Adams meeting Cinque and then drawing upon the exchange in order to make the defense case before the Supreme Court have been discounted by a number of critics as historically inaccurate. Adams and Cinque never met; Adams's actual presentation before the Court took more than eight hours over two days and focused primarily on condemning the political nature of President Martin Van Buren's interference in the defendants' right to due process of law. This critique, while justified historically, ignores how this development of crisis into climax is a logical culmination of the film's narrative structure. By providing words for his final (and successful) defense, the cinematic Cinque, through his representatives, demonstrates that articulation allows empowerment.

The presentation of Adams's Supreme Court speech parallels a comparable climax moment in *Schindler's List,* Spielberg's previous film, when Oskar Schindler addresses his assembled factory workers before he flees from the invading Russian army. Both scenes bring to a climax relatively unknown ("lost") stories that occur within holocaust settings (Freedman B7). Both present speeches of self-definition. The moments in both cases show that central male characters have undergone a process of enlightenment and change; their commitment necessitates the speeches they articulate. Schindler, on the verge of becoming a victim himself, agonizes to those he has saved that he could have done more; Adams finds the strength to respond to the injustice of the system he and his own father have helped build. Both scenes are addressed explicitly to the contemporary audience watching the film that presents them by suturing us into the optical point of view structure of the on-screen audience listening. Adams's speech in *Amistad* additionally allows him to turn from the row of busts to the elevated bench holding the justices of the Court, and beyond even listeners in the gallery in order to address the larger audience of history. Both speeches bring crisis to climax; they are final responses to the cruelest imaginable exploitation of victims. Both speeches ascend appropriate emotional peaks. Both speeches state explicitly, with all the clarity of melodrama, the moral issues that are at stake in their worlds. As penultimate dramatic moments in docudramas, the addresses of Spielberg's

Oskar Schindler and John Quincy Adams are rooted in historical circumstances, a rooting that argues for the instructive value of the moral perspectives they articulate. From the standpoint of docudrama, the specific historical accuracy (particularly dialogue) is secondary to the validity of the ideas the scenes argue for. Taken together, the films suggest that Spielberg as docudramatist is drawn to history as male melodrama, that is, true stories about men brought to the point where they must state moral positions defending victims of injustice.

Despite, or perhaps because of, the docudramatic logic of its argument, *Amistad* performed poorly at the U.S. box office, grossing only $44 million against production costs of $40 million. *Schindler's List,* by comparison, earned $96 million domestically against costs of $25 million (*Variety* 6–12 Apr. 1998: 11). Concerns expressed in the critical reception of the film suggest several reasons why its theatrical run reached so many fewer viewers than Spielberg's previous docudramatic effort: History, in general, and slavery, in particular, may have problematic, rather than automatic, appeal as a feature film subject area; issues of historical accuracy rendered the film's presentation suspect; and, perhaps most damaging to the box office, the publicity over the plagiarism suit brought against the film even before it was released may have damaged its credibility. These concerns are worth examining in turn.

The comparable critical and box office success of not only *Schindler's List* but also *Saving Private Ryan*[7] indicate that Spielberg has established a track record in delivering serious historical subjects to a large audience. One critic, noting the "debate over the appropriateness of a white director's presenting African American history," implies that the same kind of perception of appropriation that plagued *The Color Purple* may have dampened interest in *Amistad* (Ansen 65). Other comments by critics reflect ambivalence toward the film's presentation of the slave experience, particularly the portions of the story depicting the mutiny. The sense of cultural alienation that some critics (see above) saw as evocative of the experience of the enslaved also made the African characters inaccessible, so that the presentation of the slave as "Other" actually "fails to make a foreign culture comprehensible to [an] audience" (Shargel 62). (Inter)cultural experience points toward the complexity of the *Amistad* story. The challenge of sustaining the sense of intercultural similarity and difference extends throughout the film, culminating in the central relationship between Cinque and Adams. Conveying "the prodigious depiction of several cultures, languages, and dialects intermixing in the New World" (A. White

37) is only one element of the complexity of the narrative, which also must keep clear the conflation of political and legal issues that occurred when an American president, concerned with an upcoming election campaign, became involved in the dispensation of a court case demanding a position toward slavery.

Concerns over historical accuracy reached more than historians when Dreamworks, the producing studio, sent a free "study guide" for the film to hundreds of schools. The study guide raised concerns because it ignored the difference between fact and fabrication by encouraging students to accept created characters as historical fact (Foner A13; Leo 12; Rich A15). These objections centered on the study guide's suggested discussion of the role of the Morgan Freeman character, a composite drawn from several abolitionist figures. One critic asked, "Would we have wanted students to study black women in the Civil War South by analyzing lines delivered by Butterfly McQueen?" (Rich A15).

Questioning the film's historical validity on the basis of its main characters equates history with biography. Prior treatments of the *Amistad* episode have also used strategies of characterization to put the pre–Civil War legal and political issues it raises on an accessible, personal level. Spielberg's *Amistad* differs from its predecessors because it approaches its material on contemporary, docudramatic terms, by viewing the struggle for freedom of the *Amistad* Africans as victims progressively attaining empowerment through articulation. It makes more sense to test its validity by asking, Is "empowerment" a valid paradigm for the *Amistad* story? (And I will do so momentarily.)

The fact that the film foregrounds storytelling as a counterforce to injustice highlights the multiple ironies of writer Barbara Chase-Riboud's plagiarism charges against the film. In brief, on the basis of claims that Dreamworks had taken plot and characters from her 1987 novelization of the *Amistad* story, *Echo of Lions,* Chase-Riboud first sought an injunction to prevent the release of the film, then sued for monetary damages (Weinraub E1; *Jet* 8 Dec. 1997: 32–33; Mead 37). Dreamworks countercharged that she had lifted material from the earlier Owens novel, *Black Mutiny,* to which it had secured the rights. At bottom, one storyteller was attempting to prevent another from presenting the articulation that is the story's reason for being. Shortly thereafter, the *New York Times* charged Chase-Riboud herself with plagiarism, documenting how extensive material in one of her earlier novels, *Valide: A Novel of the Harem,* had been lifted wholesale without attribution or acknowledgment from *The Harem,* a 1936 work of nonfiction. Chase-Riboud stated she believed "reference books, encyclopedias, any kind of historical materials, are in the public domain" (Loke A34). A *New York Times* editorial responded that use of a work in the "public domain" meant only that one did not have to pay royalties for its use, a matter separate from issues of intellectual honesty and attribution of material (Klinkenborg A18).[8]

Shortly afterward, Chase-Riboud dropped her lawsuit. Beyond opportunism and self-promotion, it is possible to view her response to the film as one impelled by an understandable sense of appropriation. It is not simply a matter of Spielberg getting the biggest audience. Chase-Riboud's version allows its black characters to be more engaged in story events than does any other *Amistad* narrative. A fictional black abolitionist character named Braithwaite supports the defense. James Covey is developed as a hero and a romantic interest for Braithwaite's daughter, Vivian. Cinque and the others of his group are far more articulate much earlier and contribute more to their defense; Cinque's experiences are presented directly, rather than filtering his point of view, as the film does, through Baldwin, Covey, and Adams, all English-speaking interlocutors. In Chase-Riboud's telling, black characters are more directly responsible for their own story.

To pursue the possibility that Spielberg has (ironically) appropriated a story of empowerment, it is worth noting the way that John Quincy Adams, a white elder statesman, essentially "takes over" the story as the film narrative progresses from crisis to climax. Arguably, what Spielberg has done by making the film is comparable. This position, however, equates appropriation with mediation. Neither Adams nor Spielberg tells the story as their own, but instead both ensure that it reaches important audiences. Rather than appropriate the story, it is more accurate to say that Adams and Spielberg help complete its telling.

Clearly, the question then becomes one of whether or not *Amistad* truly is a story of empowerment. Do the Africans the story is about gain power in any sense? Have they freed themselves? Consider first the negative: The film's ending tries to suggest empowerment has occurred by showing the group of free(d) Africans on a ship, returning to Africa, as a direct consequence of the Supreme Court decision. The cinematic transition elides the year the group spent waiting to leave, laboring for wages, and laboring at religious lessons so that it would return as converts, missionaries representing their sponsor. Have they articulated their case? Spielberg (contrary to the historical record) has Adams and Cinque meet in order to suggest that what emerged was a collaboration of equals, so that Adams presents Cinque's case. The film shows a white elder statesman finishing the story—because he speaks the story becomes his, so that even his ancestors, not Cinque's, occupy the pictorial and figurative background of his speech. All *Amistad* narratives agree that the story becomes centered on John Quincy Adams as the trial moves to the Supreme Court, where the main issues for Adams were not slavery but the Van Buren administration's interference in judicial process and its misuse of American treaties. Did the case of the *Amistad* Africans strike a blow against legalized slavery in the United States? Several years after their decision in the *Amistad* matter, a majority of the same justices would in fact uphold, in the Dred Scott decision, the legality of American slavery.

The counterargument to these observations, grounded as they are in historical consensus, is that they confuse "power" with "empowerment," particularly as the notion of "empowerment" has meaning for the late-1990s audience the film was made for. "Empowerment" means primarily "to invest with power," according to the 1971 *Compact Edition of the Oxford English Dictionary;* contemporary culture adds the sense that individuals can in fact enable themselves. The *Amistad* Africans became empowered, first, when they freed themselves from their chains and took up knives and, again, when they became litigants in the American courts. Their empowerment then entailed not only liberation but also recognition. True, their case did not overturn America's pre–Civil War slavery laws. What it did instead was to force American courts to acknowledge their status as autonomous human beings rather than property.

It is in this most fundamental respect that Spielberg tells the *Amistad* story. The film adapts the history of what Adams (and the rest) said and did as a series of encounters necessitating a progressive recognition and acknowledgment of human worth. As a docudrama, *Amistad* shows the passage its characters undergo from victimization to trial and articulation. As a docudrama, the film foregrounds the emotional import of the story against the background of its political and legal history. As a docudrama, the film persuades us to see, far more clearly than we might otherwise, moral truth within this true story.

The 1999 Feature Film Docudramas

Despite the wide range of subjects addressed in the cycle of feature film docudramas released in the United States in 1999, all of these films center on the problem of ambition. The films explore equally the benefits and the costs of ambition for their main characters, their families, and their communities. They explore aspirations that range from the enlightened medicine practiced in *Patch Adams* to the cello mastery of Jackie DuPre in *Hilary and Jackie.* Two key arguments emerge from the 1999 cycle's treatment of ambition and suggest the timeliness of these films for their audiences: The desire for self-determination fuels ambition, and the rituals that allow for and demonstrate the redemption of ambition are empowering.

Docudramas adapt the character/conflict/closure components of classic Hollywood narrative form into configurations of victims, the trials they undergo, and moments that articulate the meanings of those trials. The 1999 features portray their real-life principals as potential victims of their own ambitions. The literal and figurative trials they undergo demonstrate what those ambitions cost. Their case studies become exemplary, as they provide their audiences opportunities to reflect upon relatable, individual needs, such as purpose, support, and community affirmation, as well as ability and accomplishment. In each case, the resolution of the conflicts that ambitions create clarifies the terms of redemption. Closure in these stories works to redeem ambition and its costs. The films articulate the redemption of ambition in varyingly visual ways (the butterfly in *Patch Adams;* the Carnegie Hall concert in *Music of the Heart;* the final rocket launch in *October Sky*), so that a basic thrust of the stories' arguments is to suggest that redemption is warranted not only by the actual events that motivate their telling as feature films but also through the physical, temporal, and spatial components that culminate in their telling. Community participation provides a final, key component of the way that action articulates the redemptive value of ambition. The best ambitions, the films argue, are those that make the world a better place for everyone, not simply those who are ambitious.

The ambition of the real-life principals here is their main virtue. Ambition at its most basic is a desire to achieve, to accomplish goals. By definition, ambition creates necessary opposition to a starting point. Ambitions arise both because of and in spite of their roots, their culture of origination, and, consequently, can become a source of resentment. If "virtue" is purity of soul, these people are "pure" in part because of their single-minded desires to pursue difficult, possibly insurmountable goals that alienate them from their families and communities. We see this in Jan Schlichtmann's advocacy for small town victims against large corporate polluters in *Civil Action;* Jackie DuPre's musicianship in *Hilary and Jackie;* Roberta Guaspari's need to teach in *Music of the Heart;* Virgil Adamson's pursuit of substance despite the distractions of being able to see in *At First Sight;* and the rocket boys' need to make their creations fly in *October Sky.* Ambition assumes an aura of accomplishment in these films when the possibilities arise of changing for the better not only the lives of the principals but also the lives of those around them. The films argue that their ambitions are both self-centered and selfless. Patch Adams and Roberta Guaspari attract attention to themselves because they challenge and change institutional patterns in pursuing their desires to improve the state of what they do; Homer Hickham is much like any kid who wants to play with his toys, but he ends up involving most of his hometown in the game, because they see in his rocketry experiments the possibility of accomplishments (rockets that work, success in science fairs, a chance to go to college) that will allow a life outside of Coalwood and its customary life sentence of working as a coal miner.

The ambitions these films tell of are not without costs. At the least, the real-life principals are presented to us as people whose unconventional obsessions put at risk the ways their communities perceive them. At the worst, the problematic nature of their ambitions victimizes them and their supporters. They are risk takers; risks are necessary if redemption is to be the eventual reward. Jan Schlichtmann, in *A Civil Action,* for example, becomes progressively possessed by the Woburn case. It takes over his attention, his practice, and his life, while his partners watch and comment but are unable to make him alter the course that will put them out of business. Eventually, Schlichtmann's offices are empty, devoid of furniture, staff, and clients (see fig. 27). The people telling us their stories in these films become alienated from their peers because of their ambitions. Their divergence from the norm makes their rationality questionable. A principal's sense of direction, of "vision," isolates but also elevates while providing the focus that his or her supporters need. Roberta Guaspari empties her house when she fires the men working on renovating it. She sheds her boyfriend out of the same necessity, since the men are creating compromises that she does not feel she must live with. Her students, like Jan Schlichtmann's Woburn clients, must depend upon the single-mindedness that will make it possible to reach otherwise inaccessible goals. On the other hand, in each case, such focused dedication would be impossible without the support network provided by those closest to the story's real-life principal. Roberta creates her work because she needs a job to feed and clothe her children; Patch Adams turns his med school friends into coworkers at his clinic; Jackie depends upon sister Hilary to such an extreme that she is allowed to sleep with her brother-in-law as a way to bolster her failing self-esteem; Hurricane Carter is freed from prison with the help of his Canadian "family"; Homer Hickham has the benefit of not only his fellow rocket boys but also an encouraging science teacher, machinists at his father's coal mine who can create rocket parts to specifications, and an infinitely understanding mother who can mediate the division growing between father and son.

The force of convention in these films acts consistently to oppose the desires of ambition. Antagonists assume the form of established, conventional, often explicitly patriarchal figures of repression. Patch Adams early on runs afoul of the dean of his medical school, who forbids lower-level medical students access to patients in the school's hospital. Jan's opposing counsel is an equally crotchety older male lawyer, who, like Adams's med school dean, directs his authoritative air of experience through the conventions of his work, clothing, briefcase, pens, and work space. Hilary's promising career as a musician is derailed when she is still a student by one of her professors, a horrifically rigid technician who destroys ambition with a few cutting comments. Homer's rocket work is viewed with suspicion by the principal of his school, who eagerly supports the prosecution of the boys when it appears that they have started a forest fire with one of their launches. His father, John, condemns their rocketry because he opposes anything that will divert his son from their shared fate, a life devoted to the Olga coal mine. As the mine's manager, he forbids the boys to have any scrap material and cuts off their access to borrowed labor by putting Mr. Bykovsky, the first machinist to help them, back into the mine (where he is eventually killed in a collapse). When John is himself injured in a subsequent accident, it forces Homer to have to take over the obligation of providing for the family by working in the mine. The abuses of their power sometimes renders the key antagonists in these films corrupt as well as repressive. Hurricane Carter apparently is victimized from the time he is a teenager by the same bad cop. Schlichtmann's legal opponents in *A Civil Action* appear to have the advantages of size, resources, and eventually even the predisposition of the judge, who is solely responsible for deciding the Woburn case.

As opposition to ambition escalates, the principals in each of these films are put through a successive series of trials. In some instances the trials are literal legal processes, such as the hearings to prove liability in *A Civil Action,* the appeals in *The Hurricane,* or the reprimands that become official proceedings brought against Patch Adams to eject him from medical school. In other films, the trials are more figurative: Jackie DuPre becomes increasingly stressed (and distressed) by the extensive traveling that takes her as a professional performer away from her family. Recurring close-ups of her cello case, traveling from stop to stop on wheels, suggest that it is the instrument that plays the musician, rather than the other way around. Roberta Guaspari must re-prove the value of her teaching methods periodically in concerts that demonstrate that she has turned children into musicians, culminating in a final concert to attempt to raise enough funds to continue her program (a concert in Carnegie Hall, no less, in a climax that places students from throughout the years of her teaching career performing on stage alongside Isaac Stern, Itzhak Perlman, and other, notable professional musicians who support her cause). The films show that risk is risky: Taking risks creates trials and jeopardizes ambition itself. Patch Adams risks his student status (and his chance to have the career he has dreamed of and worked for) by breaking institutional rules. His girlfriend is killed as a result of her work for his clinic, forcing the issue of whether or not his actions are responsible. Homer risks social ostracism for investing his energy in rockets rather than football; like Patch Adams, he breaks rules (of family, school, and mining company) to pursue his dream; also, like Patch Adams, Jan Schlichtmann, and Hurricane Carter, he suffers when others near to him are victimized for risks he has encouraged them to take.

The trials in these films place people, their ambitions, and the risks they incur on public display. Without risk there is no reward; however, these films go further by arguing that the risks taken for a worthy goal redeem the costs of the main characters' single-minded ambitions. By positioning community members as witnesses to these trials, the films make visible what ambition means. The recurrence of witness configurations instructs a film audience by aligning us with the audience, the witnesses on screen; the public display of the consequences of ambition also validates risks taken for a greater good. The fact that Homer's rocket launches always run the risk of failure seems to draw progressively larger crowds of spectators. In the hearing scene in *Patch Adams,* the gallery is crowded with patients, nurses, fellow medical students, and faculty, suggesting all are invested in the board's verdict on Patch's anti-empirical, humanistic approach to medical practice (see fig. 28). Similarly, both jail staff as well as prosecuting police officers are present at Hurricane Carter's final hearing. The verdicts of these trials argue that ambition is redeemed to the extent that accomplishment exceeds self-interest.

The successive trials that provide the basic dramatic structure for these films allow opportunities to prove that the risks of ambition are worthwhile and, as a matter of narrative resolution, to signify accomplishment.

The obstacles erected and the trials that ensue define the risks necessitated by ambition. The main characters' abilities to navigate their literal or figurative trials become an indicator of their determination and wherewithal. The risks of ambition in these films become doubly warranted. They not only are based on actuality but also are shown to us as inscribed within the visual fields of their historical and social contexts. This double warranting of risk and reward allows these docudramas to articulate the value of the risks that have placed their real-life principals in positions of jeopardy. *October Sky* provides a fruitful case study in the anchoring of ambition in the visible.

As a docudrama, *October Sky* inscribes its real material within two melodramatic contexts, the social and the familial. This film, like the others in the group of 1999 features, argues that ambition allows self-determination and shows how self-determination operates within social and familial realms. What is specific to *October Sky* is that at key moments in the film, imagery of constraint (associated with the state of being earthbound, suggestive of the influence of familial and social expectations) contrasts with the goals of ambition, conveyed through imagery of flight and freedom set within or against the sky. This image system is evident throughout the film; however, I will discuss its functions in specific scenes set in the Hickham house, the coal mine, Homer's school, and the launch pad the boys build on the mountainside. The film's systematic visual interrelationship of settings, constraints, and the need for self-determination helps the accessibility of its arguments about ambition, lending those arguments a strongly affective appeal.

I am using the phrase "self-determination" to refer to the general desirability for any individual to have the freedom to act independently from external constraints. The settings of family home, school, and workplace become in film melodrama logical sites for the conflict of social codes and individual desires. *October Sky* shows the groundedness of these settings conflicting directly with Homer's ambitions to create and launch rockets, as I shall show in my discussion of the film. The action of social contexts opposing individual ambition and fueling self-determination forms the core of the rhetoric of *October Sky*. The film uses the 1950s (and 1960s) to make a case for the importance of empowerment for its primary (1999) audience. Self-determination is bound to be an effective, appealing argument for an audience already familiar with the rhetoric of empowerment. For many viewing the film in its initial release, "empowerment" would be aligned with the most positive cultural values, and an established part of the Clinton administration's political rhetoric regarding economic self-determination. The film's arguments for self-determined ambition become immediately accessible to this late-1990s audience through the bundle of signifiers the setting evokes. The time (the late 1950s) and the location of the story (Coalwood, a small mining community in the mountains of West Virginia) allow for a full, emphatic staging of conventions, exposing the historical and social determinants at work on the story's characters. *October Sky*'s evocation of times gone by did not pass unnoticed by critics who compared the film's use of the past to the presentation of peer group influence in *Stand By Me* (Maslin, "Eyes Toward" E14), the politics of small town ambition in *Hoosiers* (Millar 1), and the inspirational force of a 1960s kind of idealism in *Field of Dreams* (Maher 60). The function of the past setting in the film is not to embrace the safety of nostalgia so much as it is to expose the visibility of historical and social constraints influencing the characters in the world of the film. The launch of Sputnik situates story events within the period of the Cold War, recalling specifically the connected, competitive impetus the launch provided both to the U.S. space program and to the need for American education to "step up" to meet the challenge the race for space had created. If Sputnik signifies the historical pressure to achieve that was born from historical events in 1957, the small town setting of the film evokes all the conflicting pressures to conform that could oppose ambition. Once seeded by Homer's dream to launch rockets of their own, the "Rocket Boys" as a social group forms emphatically both within and in spite of pressure from peer groups, families, and the larger Coalwood community. Underlying the pressure to conform in the world of the film is the reality of a life that is entirely dependent upon the economy of coal mining. The film translates economic pressures into familial tensions, into the pressure for sons to be like each other and their father, and into the subversive support afforded to Homer by his mother. The contrasting historical and social pressures that characterize *October Sky*'s setting allow for the visibility of constraints on Homer and his friends. The film's critics responded enthusiastically to the way "the film recreates an era when a can-do spirit was an American birthright" (Strickler OE1), noting equally that the small mining town setting and its "dispiriting bits of physical life" could allow "the emotions of the story—wild hopes of adventure and flight—[to] jump out like shooting stars" (Denby, "Popular Mechanic" 184). The strains made so emphatic in the film's setting set up a logical narrative arc of self-determining character desire. The presence of the community means that "we want to know how he did it, how he overcame skepticism and failure" (Carr D4).

An early scene of the film shows the seed of Homer's ambition in the basic juxtaposition of earth, home, and sky: the people of Coalwood, including Homer, stand on the porches of their houses and gaze upward in awe, watching Sputnik, a tiny blinking light that arcs steadily across the stars. Later in the film, in a moment explicitly recalling the film's opening, Homer stands on the tipple, the platform that is about to take him down into the coal mine, where he must go to work because his father has been injured. As the descent begins and he looks up and through the wire mesh enclosing the platform, we see the same shot of Sputnik that opened the film. The satellite is there once more, visible momentarily before the elevator begins to drop into the darkness below. The scenes contrast each other as they put the possible in flight within the presence of the constrained, earthbound actual. Homer's first launches (from the yard of his house) extend this association by bringing his rocket dreams into direct collision with the material reality of home and work. His first rocket explodes, destroying a section of their fence, a fence (like the house itself) built and owned by the Olga company. Another rocket launched soon afterward flies into the side of the coal mine office, resulting in a direct mandate from his father to stop launching rockets and to stop using company materials to make them.

Home and work in the coal mine appear in direct opposition to the possibilities the sky holds. The Hickham house is an extension of the mine, since John, Homer's father, manages the mine's operation and must embody the male authority of both work and home. Homer's mother works perpetually on a large mural on one wall that shows her dream of escape, an expanse of beach and ocean, further underlining the contrast between the ideal of freedom and open air and the reality of work and home. The mine is right across the street. John and everyone else who goes into the mine emerges with face and clothing blackened by coal dust. A black telephone in the living room of the Hickham house is a direct line to the mine office. It rings constantly, drawing John into taut conversations that lead to his abruptly stomping off to solve a steady stream of work problems. The calls tend to interrupt family dinners and conversations that compare Homer to his brother, Jim, who plays football for his high school. Jim's escape is ensured. He will go to college on a football scholarship. Without a similar accomplishment, Homer's future in Coalwood holds only the prospect of work like his father's, in the mine. Homer's hopes to escape the mine depend upon the intellectual accomplishment that rocketry might make possible.

The Hickham home is a site of several basic oppositions, as work intrudes upon domestic space: Paternal and maternal values clash; work and education are viewed as divergent futures; the future of the older brother may exclude a similar possibility for the younger. The social codes that make domestic space contradictory in the film also pertain to Homer's life at school. School life shows Homer as inappropriately earthbound. He tries out for the football team and is encouraged by the coach to use his determination in a less self-destructive way. In another early scene in the school, Homer crosses the cafeteria to talk to Quentin, who sits alone because he is a nerd, an intellectual, and thus an outcast. Quentin represents knowledge, however, specifically the possibility of knowing what it will take to make successful rockets. When Homer sits down with Quentin, the storm of looks and whispers that results suggests that he, too, risks becoming shunned. Homer's choice indicates how the strength of his commitment to his dream overpowers his concerns for social constraints in Coalwood. He has his chemistry teacher, Miss Riley, as a supporter of his ambition, but Mr. Turner, the principal of the school, appears skeptical, if not outright antagonistic (he accuses the rocket boys of being "bomb builders"). His doubts appear to be confirmed (and the future of rocketry in complete doubt) when the boys are called to his office and confronted with an accusation by the state police that one of their rockets has caused a forest fire. Subsequently, when the rocket that has caused the fire is produced, it is Mr. Turner, however, who is instrumental in exonerating the boys' claims of innocence. He confirms that what they are looking at is an aviation flare fired from a nearby air base. Found innocent, the boys now receive his full support for their efforts to enter their rockets in the science fair, which may lead to national recognition and a college scholarship.

Community and its commentary on Homer's ambitions become ubiquitous in *October Sky*. The function of community and familial and social constraints in the film is articulated fully in the scene of the launch of the boys' last rocket. They have saved their biggest rocket for last; the launch attracts the largest crowd yet of onlookers, including John, after he's resisted Homer's invitations throughout the film to come see their rockets; the rising rocket is visible from all points in the community, including the window of Miss Riley's hospital room (see figs. 29–33). The size and power of the launch suggest how the rockets throughout the film have been emblems as well as embodiments of Homer's aspirations, arguing that ambition steeled by idealism can punch through the limitations it faces. The rockets have had a bandwagon effect, leading from the few (like Mr. Bykovsky, the machinist) who have supported Homer's ambitions to become the many (when Homer needs the help of townspeople and mine workers to replace the parts of his science fair exhibit that have been stolen at the national fair in Indianapolis) to this final suggestion that "everyone" is not only on board but also touched and, therefore, has benefited from the scale of Homer's ambitions. Community presence in the scene redeems Homer's ambitions as much as does the successful launch of this most spectacular of all his rockets. The number, the range, and the multiplicity of viewpoints of witnesses reinforce the public nature of the accomplishment and the sense that this has happened not just for the rocket boys but for everyone. Town support has built slowly; a small but growing number have come to watch past launches; the town has pitched together to help get Homer's exhibits to the national science fair, though no one is able to go there to see him win. Now Coalwood shares directly the fruits of Homer's ambition. The risks taken in such an extreme departure from the norm have paid proportionate dividends. For the first time, John appears at a launch. John's presence suggests that he has overcome the ambivalence that has led him to forbid Homer's rocketry yet allow him to have scrap materials from the mine and the use of the mine's property for a launch site. "A rocket won't fly unless someone pushes the button," Homer says, inviting his father to be a direct part of this last achievement, and so John steps forward. The comparison of boy, sources of ambition, father/son relations, and rocket flight is complete.

As the rocket thunders upward, it appears visible from a number of vantage points throughout Coalwood, affirming its centrality to the community. Most notably, we see it framed in the window of Miss Riley's hospital room. The framing defines the flight and its sense of accomplishment as in part hers, endorsing not only the ambition of the student but also the selfless work of the teacher in helping to realize that ambition. The shot offers a final coupling of the earthbound, the hospital, the sickbed, and the limits of the present, with the sky, and with the possibilities afforded by hope and faith in dreams. The view encapsulates in one image the action of rockets mediating real and ideal, starting point and goal, and earth and heaven, which has been systematic throughout the film.

Conclusion: Docudramatic Strategies of Articulation

A central reason to approach discourse rhetorically is to examine how expression extends itself to its audience. In its blending of documentary material and melodramatic narrative form, docudrama emphasizes its strategies of articulation, because these, in the fashion of melodrama, articulate the moral meaning of the material of the real that has impelled the story being told.

The group of feature film docudramas I have examined here indicate three kinds of strategies of articulation at work. Most prominent is the victim/trial configuration that structures these narratives. Trials anchor a subject in the actuality of public record. As do the hearings in *Call Northside, Quiz Show, JFK, In the Name of the Father,* and many MOWs, these trials also provide a forum for articulation, showcasing the presentation of reasons for thoughts and behaviors. The very concept of a trial, whether literal or figurative, allows for illustrating the interplay of justice and injustice. The verdict in any trial is momentous because as a film shows outcome shedding light on matters of right and wrong, it recalibrates the moral compass of our world.

My discussion has drawn attention to a second strategy these particular films have used advantageously, that is, the cinematic figuring of absence. Absence reminds. By referring us to what is missing, absence makes present the accomplishment of survival and its costs. When a film such as *13 Rue Madeleine* or *Shannon Mohr* shows us what survival is worth and why it is worthwhile, it argues how the singular perspective of a particular story provides moral clarity. We have reasons why someone's story should be exemplary.

The reformulation of conventions that *Rosewood* makes problematic is shared, although to a less emphatic degree, by the other films in this group and suggests a third articulation strategy. Joining *Rosewood*'s black hero as a Western action figure in a small Southern town is the *Amistad* group's own leader providing moral guidance to the process of American government; the white lawyer as a black hero in *Ghosts;* the psychologically re-treaded artist of *Shine* finding fulfillment not in solipsistic creative activity but, instead, in extending himself in his relationships with his audience; the depiction of Larry Flynt, pornographer, as a civil rights and First Amendment advocate; and Joe Pistone's Donnie Brasco, struggling with the moral dilemma he creates for himself when he must do bad things for a good cause, and when he finds a surprising amount of good in the criminal he is sworn to bring to justice. When told docudramatically, the stories of these individuals reshape the traditional, conventional roles of cop, pornographer, artist, lawyer, hero, and slave. The departures from the traditional iconography of any of these roles also helps articulate the costs of survival, whether it be through Pistone's check for services rendered, Flynt's desires reduced to pornographic necrophilia, Helfgott's idiosyncratic expressions of love for those who confirm his gifts, Myrlie Evers's comment that in his struggles on her behalf, DeLaughter "reminds" her of Medgar, or Cinque's ironically empty triumphant return to Africa as a free man.

Docudrama is susceptible to the charge that its real material becomes distorted when it is filtered through the narrative structures of Hollywood feature film form. This group of recent feature films illustrates how this susceptibility grows out of the rhetorical functions of docudrama. As rhetorical projects, the films extend persuasive arguments to their audiences. In pursuing their rhetorical missions, they depart from their representation of the real. Consequently, *Rosewood* requires the fiction of Mr. Mann to embody the collective heroism of its holocaust survivors, *Ghosts* becomes the story of the lawyer, rather than the client, and *Amistad* allows Cinque and John Quincy Adams the chance to meet so that Adams's actual eight-hour oration to the Supreme Court on the misapplication of law in the case becomes, in order to be relatable to its audience, a several minute appeal to the very basis of America's foundation in recognizing the inherent worth of human beings. Our obligation is to understand how, as these works "based on true stories" address us, they have stated, clearly and directly, that what they represent contributes to discourse about our history and our culture precisely because it has been put to rhetorical purpose.

APPENDIXES
NOTES
WORKS CITED
INDEX

Appendix 1

Docudramas Aired During Sweeps Periods, 1994–1997

Sweeps Period	Movies of the Week	
	Docudrama	Total
September 1994	35 (11.95)	293
October 1994	20 (6.51)	307
January 1995	26 (9.06)	287
September 1995	53 (16.67)	318
October 1995	47 (15.99)	294
January 1996	37 (11.60)	319
September 1996	30 (11.90)	252
October 1996	21 (6.86)	306
January 1997	28 (8.67)	323
Average	(11.02)	

Note: Numbers in parentheses are percentages.

Appendix 2

Annotated Script Page (*Princess in Love*)

PRINCESS IN LOVE

FADE IN: ~~#62~~

Actual interview INT. KENSINGTON PALACE - DRAWING ROOM - DAY

Dialogue slightly paraphrased and condensed Stunning PRINCESS DIANA, 34, is subdued, regal in a Navy blue suit, gold earrings. She's being interviewed by the BBC for the news program, PANORAMA. (Nov. 20, 1995) #65

> DIANA
> ... I desperately loved my husband and I wanted to share everything together. I thought we were a very good team.

BBC, p.1

> INTERVIEWER
> Around 1986, Prince Charles renewed his relationship with Mrs. Camilla Parker-Bowles. Were you aware of that?

BBC, p.4

> DIANA
> Yes. But I wasn't in the position to do anything about it. I had this feeling of being no good at anything, being useless and hopeless and failed in every direction.

BBC p.4, p.5

> INTERVIEWER
> So in private, you were almost to the point of living separate lives, how did you cope in public?

BBC p.5

> DIANA
> Charles and I had our duty to perform, that was paramount.

Actual events BEGIN TITLE MONTAGE:

MUSIC ONLY: Diana and PRINCE CHARLES as the "golden couple" carrying out their official duties:

--in Rome meeting the Pope ... Dimbleby - photograph

--with rock stars at the Prince's Trust #16

--dancing together in Australia #16 ...

--at a banquet with the Reagans in Washington Dimbleby - photograph.

--kissing after a polo match #16

--in Berlin at the ballet meeting the dancers #16

145

Appendix 3
Synopsis of *Shannon Mohr*

S hannon Mohr meets Dave Davis at a friend's wedding. After a whirl-wind courtship, and despite the misgivings of her parents, Dave and Shannon marry and move to his farm near her hometown of Toledo, Ohio. The farm is not as big as he has led her to believe; however, he tells her he "insures everything."

They become friends with a neighboring couple; Dick and Dave are both Vietnam vets. Shannon learns from her neighbor that Dave had been married before.

Shannon's parents visit often enough that Dave becomes resentful. One morning they argue as Bob and Lucille Mohr arrive. To smooth things over, Dave suggests they go for a horseback ride. Shortly after they leave, he gallops up to Dick, who is working in one of his fields. Shannon has fallen from her horse.

Dick and Dave rush her to a hospital. Dave tells the police he has no insurance for Shannon. As the Mohrs arrive, they learn that Shannon has died. Lucille Mohr notices scratches on Dave's face.

Dave insists that Shannon's wishes were to be cremated. Her mother and father protest vehemently that it could not be what she wanted because she was raised a Catholic. Dick takes their side. Dave backs off; however, Shannon's body is prepared for burial before an autopsy can be performed.

The next morning Dave asks Dick if he would be interested in buying his property. The Mohrs soon learn that Dave is receiving payoffs on at least six life insurance policies he had taken out on Shannon.

Dick leads the police to the spot where Shannon fell. They find one of her shoes on the ground, unlaced.

At Shannon's funeral, Dave's mother tells Bob Mohr that her son was never in the army, let alone in Vietnam.

Dave picks up Jeri, an old girlfriend, and leaves for Florida.

The Mohrs insist on an inquest. Circumstantial evidence leads to a conclusion of accidental death. A reporter for a Detroit newspaper questions the lack of an investigation. He tracks down Dave Davis's previous wife, who claims Davis tried to beat her to death.

The Mohrs convince Brooks, an investigator in the district attorney's office, to look into their daughter's death. They agree to have the body exhumed. There are no traces of blood or skin under her fingernails.

In Florida, Davis buys false identity papers. He has a boat and appears to be living with yet another woman.

Traces of Pentactin, a paralyzing drug, turn up in Shannon's tissue samples. Brooks has her body exhumed yet again, and puncture marks are found on her body.

Davis escapes the country before he can be apprehended.

Six years go by. Brooks decides to try to reopen the case by presenting it as an episode of *Unsolved Mysteries*. A number of phone calls fail to turn up Dave Davis. The program is rerun a year later. A new tip leads to Davis's capture in American Samoa.

Davis is tried and convicted of Shannon Mohr's murder.

Notes

Preface: Based on a True Story

1. See, for example, Richard M. Barsam, *Nonfiction Film: A Critical History* (New York: Dutton, 1973): 14, 22–23, 79; see also Erik Barnouw, *Documentary: A History of the Non-Fiction Film* (New York: Oxford UP, 1984): 26, 61, 144–48, 309–15.

2. The next chapter examines how studies of the historical film have treated docudrama; see also Custen *(Bio/Pics)*. Tuska 192–95 and Hirsh 172–73 view the turn toward location cinematography in postwar "semidocumentaries" as part of the urban aesthetic that characterizes film noir.

3. Alan Rosenthal notes that "of the 115 movies shown on TV in the first broadcast season of 1992, 43 were docudramas." He notes also that "in the overall 1991 TV season, seven out of the top ten highest-rated movies made for TV were based on real-life happenings" *(Writing* 9). My own data on MOW docudrama distribution suggest that 11 percent of the network and cable MOWs broadcast from 1994 to 1997 were docudramas (see chap. 5).

4. This model of argument was developed originally by British logician Stephen Toulmin in *The Uses of Argument* (Cambridge: Cambridge UP, 1958).

5. Chapter 2 details the three kinds of warrants at work in docudrama: models (depending wholly on resemblance to their referents), sequences (actual and re-created images precede and/or follow one another), and interactions (actual and re-created elements appear together simultaneously on screen).

6. The nature of postmodernist history is that it signposts (indicates) its own processes of representation. As a conventional narrative form, docudrama avoids the self-conscious discourse characteristic of postmodernist history. Signposting does occur in docudrama through, for example, explanatory titles that clarify sources of material, and contextual cues that distinguish traditionally fictional from non-fictional modes of presentation (distribution and exhibition of a work as a feature film, for example, rather than as a televised half-hour public affairs program).

1. Defining Docudrama: *Schindler's List* and *In the Name of the Father*

1. This is a representative but by no means exhaustive survey. For a detailed, thorough etymology, see Derek Paget, *No Other Way to Tell It: Dramadoc/Docudrama in Television* (Manchester: Manchester UP, 1998): 90–115.

2. With regard to the compound terms he is defining, Paget has a relevant observation:

> It is tempting to regard the phrases, however they appear typographically, as always weighted towards the second word. Thus, just as "dramatic" in the phrase "dramatic documentary" acts as an adjective modifying the noun "documentary," so "drama documentary" acts as an adjective modifying the noun "documentary," so "dramadocumentary" is a documentary treated dramatically. But "drama-documentary" claims a balance in which, perhaps, both will be equally present. (93)

3. See Robert Burgoyne, "Temporality as Historical Argument in Bertolucci's *1900*," *Cinema Journal* 28.3 (1989): 57–68; her ideas (and his answer to her response) appear in *Cinema Journal* 29.3 (1990): 69–78.

4. Peirce's language in describing the index is noteworthy in that he pursues the relationship of icon and index accordingly:

> An *Index* is a sign which refers to the Object that it denotes by virtue of being really affected by that Object. . . . In so far as the Index is affected by the Object, it necessarily has some Quality in common with the Object, and it is in respect to these that it refers to the Object. It does, therefore, involve a sort of Icon, although an Icon of a peculiar kind; and it is not the mere resemblance of its Object, even in these respects which makes it a sign, but it is the actual modification of it by the Object. (102)

To rephrase, the signifier not only necessarily "refers" to its signified but the signified also acts upon and/or changes ("affects," "modifies") its own signifier. Applied to docudrama, the "action" of original events conceivably includes the evolution of their retelling and reformulation.

5. "Warrants indicate how, given the available grounds, it [is] reasonable for the listener or reader to make the inferential leap from them to the claim. . . . Warrants are found in things already accepted as true as a part of common knowledge, values, customs, and societal norms" (Rybocki and Rybocki 52).

6. Thomas Keneally, *Schindler's List* (New York: Simon and Schuster, 1982); Gerry Conlon, *In the Name of the Father* (New York: Plume, 1993)—published originally as *Proved Innocent* (London: Hamilton, 1990); and Jim Garrison, *On the Trail of the Assassins* (New York: Warner, 1992). *JFK*'s credits also cite Jim Marrs, *Crossfire* (New York: Carroll, 1992).

7. "Melodrama" and "domestic melodrama" have been almost interchangeable terms for scholars of film melodrama such as Charles Affron, *Cinema and Sentiment* (Chicago: U of Chicago P, 1982); and Thomas Elsaesser, "Tales of Sound and Fury," *Monogram* 4 (1972): 2–15. See also Robert Lang. According to Lang, "[T]he melodramatic imagination that structures the film understands experience in Manichean terms of familial struggle and conflict" (3).

8. In *The Melodramatic Imagination,* Peter Brooks discusses extensively the function of melodrama in a "desacralized" universe, that is, a universe otherwise lacking in moral reference (5). Melodrama's emphatic treatment and clarification of moral issues helps fill that lack.

9. *In the Name of the Father* ends in a similar fashion, relying more conventionally on an epilogic subtitle roll to update us as to the status of the actual people the film has portrayed.

2. All the Good Reasons: Persuasive Warrants and Moral Claims

1. See Stephen Toulmin, *The Uses of Argument* (Cambridge: Cambridge UP, 1958). A warrant locates the basis in common knowledge, common sense, and/or rules of logic that allow an argument to make the necessary shift from fact to value. See note 5, chapter 1.

2. In his review of semiotic theory and his overview in particular of the theory of C. S. Peirce, Peter Wollen provides the following definitions:

> An icon, according to Peirce, is a sign which represents its object mainly by its similarity to it; the relationship between signifier and signified is not arbitrary but is one of resemblance or likeness. An index is a sign by virtue of an existential bond between itself and its object. (116)

3. The 1990s have seen numerous docudrama features and television movies-of-the-week. The first few months of 1997 alone saw the release of *Rosewood, The Ghosts of Mississippi, The People Vs. Larry Flynt,* and *Donnie Brasco,* followed later in the year by *Amistad.*

4. See Richard Dyer MacCann, "The Problem Film in America," in *Film and Society,* ed. Richard Dyer MacCann (New York: Scribner's, 1964): 51–59.

5. See Jack Ellis, *The Documentary Idea* (Englewood Cliffs: Prentice-Hall, 1989): 160–62.

6. See George F. Custen, *Twentieth Century's Fox: Darryl F. Zanuck and the Culture of Hollywood* (New York: Basic Books, 1998), particularly chapters 3, 5, and 6–11.

7. Zanuck was adept at anticipating "social trends" and incorporating these concerns into TCF's adaptations (Custen, *Fox* 131).

8. Zanuck would "make films with serious themes, but wrap them in showmanship so that even as they were illuminated by their purpose and significance, people would view them as diverting and entertaining" (Custen, *Fox* 274).

9. William Lafferty's "A Reappraisal of the Semi-Documentary in Hollywood, 1945–1948," *Velvet Light Trap* 20 (Summer 1983: 22–26), provides a helpful examination of economic constraints that warranted a turn to location shooting after the war.

10. Zanuck claims credit for the effectiveness of this marriage. See Rudy Behlmer, ed., *Memo from Darryl F. Zanuck* (New York: Grove, 1993): 124.

11. TCF produced about 13 percent of Hollywood's films noirs per year from 1945 to 1949, according to data in Tuska (263–68).

12. *Newsweek* used phrasing similar to *Time's* "newsreel exactitude" (20 Jan. 1947: 92). For reference to the film's "melodrama," see *New York Times* 16 Jan. 1947: 30; also *New Republic* 27 Jan. 1947: 42. For a discussion of James Cagney's performance in relation to the story, see *Christian Science Monitor* 31 Jan. 1947: 5; *New York Times* 16 Jan. 1947: 30; and *Variety* 18 Dec. 1946: 14.

13. Regarding *House,* see *Variety* 12 Sept. 1945: 16; *Newsweek* 24 Sept. 1945: 94; *Time* 8 Oct. 1945: 96; and *Commonweal* 26 Sept. 1945: 576. For *Rue,* see *New Republic* 27 Jan. 1947: 44–45; *Variety* 18 Dec. 1946: 14; *Newsweek* 29 20 Jan. 1947: 92; *Time* 496 Jan. 1947: 89; and *Commonweal* 17 Jan. 1947: 352.

14. For a discussion of anti-Semitism and *Gentleman's Agreement,* see *New Republic* 17 Nov. 1947: 38; *Motion Picture Herald* "Product Digest" 15 Nov. 1947: 3929; and *Photoplay* Feb. 1948: 20. See also Custen, *Fox* 294. For a discussion of anti-Semitism and box office backlash, see *Commonweal* 14 Oct. 1949: 15; and *Variety* 5 Oct. 1949: 8.

15. For a discussion of the issues framing the story in *Gentlemen's Agreement,* see *New York Times* 12 Nov. 1947: 36; and *Commonweal* 21 Nov. 1947: 144. On *Gentlemen's agreement,* see also *Life* 1 Dec. 1947: 95–96; and *New Republic* 17 Nov. 1947: 38. On *Pinky,* see *Commonweal* 14 Oct. 1949: 15; *Life* 17 Oct. 1949: 112–15; and *New Republic* 3 Oct. 1949: 23.

16. See *New Republic* 17 Feb. 1947: 39.

17. See *Newsweek* 17 Mar. 1947: 100.

18. See Brooks 5. Melodrama's emphatic treatment and clarification of moral issues helps fill the lack of moral structure and allows the opportunity for moral affirmation.

19. Prologues in each case read as follows:

House:

The scenes in this picture were photographed in the localities of the incidents depicted—Washington, New York, and their vicinities; whenever possible, in the actual place the original incident occurred.

With the exception of the leading players, all F.B.I. personnel in the picture are members of the Federal Bureau of Investigation.

Rue:

No single story could ever pay full tribute to the accomplishments of the U.S. Army Intelligence in World War II. Working secretly behind enemy lines, in close cooperation with our Allies, its brilliant work was an acknowledged factor in the final victory.

In order to obtain the maximum of realism and authenticity, all the exterior and interior settings in this motion picture were photographed in the field—and wherever possible, at the actual locations.

Northside:
This is a true story.

This film was photographed in the State of Illinois using wherever possible, the actual locales associated with the story.

20. *House* features documents in almost every scene in the film. The most critical of these are the credentials of Dietrich (William Eythe), the main character. His credentials appear as a text on microfilm we see repeatedly: smuggled into the United States in a watch; projected on a screen in FBI headquarters; altered to make his mission as a double agent more effective; and then ultimately discovered to be doctored by the German spy ring he has penetrated. *House* also claims to incorporate actual FBI surveillance footage of German fifth columnists.

21. When the 077 group moves into an English country house for final training, it eats meals around a dining room table. The settings in *Rue* evolve through a number of houses, culminating in French farmhouses and the Gestapo headquarters referred to by the film's title.

22. Lassiter (Frank Latimore), one of the Americans in *Rue,* is murdered when a mole in the group, the ruthless German double agent Kunzel (Richard Conte), suspects Lassiter knows his true identity. Elsa (Signe Hasso) operates a clothing store in the front of the house on 92nd Street and also leads a cell of German agents operating out of a parlor behind one the shop's full-length mirrors. She dons a man's suit and fedora in becoming the mythic "Christopher," the head of the Nazi's entire fifth column operation.

23. Stewart confronts a series of challenges to his professional moral code, first in conveying (and eventually believing) Wiecek's story, then in unearthing the potential corruption in the judicial system that has perpetrated Wiecek's conviction, and finally in convincing his newspaper and Wiecek's parole board to support completely his efforts to bring the truth to light.

24. In the same vein, MacNeal's reportorial efforts are supported by his own wife; in brief scenes where they share a couch set up (where else?) in front of a jigsaw puzzle, she encourages him to continue to do the right things for Frank. Kelly (Lee J. Cobb), his editor, fabricates a story about his own mother scrubbing floors to put him through school as a way to keep MacNeal convinced of the rightness of pursuing the story.

25. See Kent Anderson, *Television Fraud* (Westport, CT: Greenwood, 1978); Erik Barnouw, *Tube of Plenty* (New York: Oxford UP, 1975); Thomas A. Delong, *Quiz Craze* (New York: Praeger, 1991); Walter Karp, "The Quiz-Show Scandal," *American Heritage* (May–June 1989): 88; and Michael Real, "The Great Quiz Show Scandal," *Television Quarterly* (Winter 1994: 2–27).

26. According to Karp, at least one prominent philosopher (Charles Frankel) and one political scientist (Hans Morganthau) went on record to this effect (88).

27. The film's chronology compresses the actual time frame of two years between Van Doren's competition and the testimony he gives in Washington.

28. This departure is a development of the film more so than Goodwin's book. Goodwin refers early on to a boyhood encounter when, in defending his younger brother, he ended up retaliating against an anti-Semitic taunt by one of their friends (15); he also describes Stempel's features "as bearing a dark, Semitic stamp" (69) but otherwise makes no other reference or speculation of any kind as to what the role of anti-Semitism might have been in the scandals.

3. Dramatic Evidence: Docudrama and Historical Representation

1. For an overview of traditional historiographic concerns as they pertain to the historical film, see Daniel Leab, "The Moving Image as Interpreter of History: Telling the Dancer from the Dance," in *Image as Artifact: The Historical Analysis of Film and Television,* ed. John O'Connor (Malabar, FL: Krieger, 1990): 69–95; see also Sorlin 3–66.

2. Nichols does this most extensively in *Representing Reality.*

3. See preface, note 6.

4. A brief typology of various works indicates how docudrama tends to favor "personal" subject matter, even when dealing with historical subjects. Docudrama's packaging of history falls into distinct subject categories. Frequency of production within these subtypes offers evidence of docudrama's propensity to "personalize" history.

Alan Rosenthal's *Writing Docudrama* lists eighty feature film docudramas produced and distributed since 1970 (233–34). The largest subgroup—of which there are 48—are biographies. The next largest category (of which there are 16) foregrounds social issues (stories of abuse, prejudice, and legal processes). Many of these (e.g., *Midnight Express, Reversal of Fortune,* and *In the Name of the Father*) are at least partially biographical. These are followed by groups of films (again, many of which are arguably biographies) detailing crimes and conspiracies, stories centering on music, war, and medicine and/or science. Clearly, the basic strategy of using one person's story to illuminate issues such as genocide *(The Killing Fields; Schindler's List)* or race relations *(Cry Freedom)* shows the appeal of narrativizing character desire within the referential framework of actual events.

Movie-of-the-week titles also indicate the "personal" angle of these docudramas. To illustrate the ubiquitousness of the titling pattern that places an actual name after a characterizing phrase and a colon, I open one of my university's *Educable Guides* to the movies listed for the month and need look no further than the second column to find *A Cry For Help: The Tracey Thurman Story* (1989) and *Cry in the Wild: The Taking of Peggy Ann* (1991).

5. Sorlin sees several kinds of time at work in historical film. Historical time (the past) is presented through chronological time as well as the symbolic significance of important dates (moments) in history, such as July 4, 1776. These various senses of time may run within and without story time, which Sorlin breaks down into conventional categories such as "shortened" and "elongated" time as it is narrated. His typology avoids dealing directly with subjective experiences

of time. What I am calling "personal" time is an intersection of symbolic and story time (56–59). His discussion is similar to the exchange about temporal duration between Robert Burgoyne and Angela Dalle-Vacche that I cite above in chapter 1, note 3.

4. Docudrama Ethics and the Problem of Proximity

1. See, for example, Gerald R. Ford and David W. Belin, "The Kennedy Assassination: How about the Truth?" *Washington Post National Weekly* 23 Dec. 1991; Roger Hilsman, "How Kennedy Viewed the Vietnam Conflict," *New York Times* 20 Jan. 1992; Leslie H. Gelb, "Kennedy and Vietnam," *New York Times* 6 Jan. 1992; William Manchester, "No Evidence for a Conspiracy to Kill Kennedy," *New York Times* 5 Feb. 1992; David W. Belin, "Oswald Was a Lone Gunman," *Wall Street Journal* 16 Jan. 1992, and "Earl Warren's Assassins," *New York Times* 7 Mar. 1992; Bernard Weinraub, "Valenti Denounces Stone's *JFK* as a 'Smear,'" *New York Times* 14 Apr. 1992; and Stone's response to many of the above in "The JFK Assassination—What about the Evidence?" *Washington Post National Weekly* 5 Jan. 1992, and in "The Shooting of JFK, Stone's interview with R. S. Anson, in *Esquire* Nov. 1991.

2. These include Tom Wicker, "Does *JFK* Conspire Against Reason?" *New York Times* 15 Dec. 1991; Kenneth Auchincloss, "Twisted History," *Newsweek* 23 Dec. 1991; Tom Bethell, "Conspiracy to End Conspiracies," *National Review* 16 Dec. 1991; John Leo, "Oliver Stone's Paranoid Propaganda," *U.S. News and World Report* 13 Jan. 1992; and Lance Morrow, "When Artists Distort History," *Time* 23 Dec. 1991.

3. See Anson (note 1 above); also Edward J. Epstein, "The Second Coming of Jim Garrison," *Atlantic Monthly* Mar. 1993.

4. David Ansen, "What Does Oliver Stone Owe History?" *Newsweek* 23 Dec. 1991; Richard Corliss, "Who Killed JFK?" *Time* 23 Dec. 1991.

5. According to Janet Maslin ("Oliver Stone"):

> Images fly by breathlessly and without identification. Composite characters are intermingled with actual ones. Real material and simulated scenes are intercut in a deliberately bewildering fashion. The camera races bewilderingly across supposedly "top secret" documents and the various charts and models being used to explain forensic evidence. Major matters and petty ones are given equal weight. Accusations are made by visual implication rather than rational deduction, as when the camera fastens on an image of Lyndon Johnson while a speaker uses the phrase "coup d'etat."

6. See Rosenthal on "signposting" (*Writing* 205–6).

5. Rootable, Relatable, Promotable Docudrama: The MOW Mantra as Rhetorical Practice

1. Alan Rosenthal confirms that in 1991, 43 out of 115 TV movies were

docudramas (*Writing* 9). See also appendix 1 for the percentages of docudramas shown during prime time over the last two years.

2. There are literally hundreds of examples of these films, with warranted credibility because they are based on events rooted in the news; my personal favorite remains *The Positively True Adventures of the Alleged Texas Cheerleader-Murdering Mom* (1993), in which, as described by my local cable guide, "A Texas mother hires a killer to off her daughter's rival."

3. See appendix 2 for an example of an annotated script page from *Princess in Love*. In this case, "BBC" refers to a transcript of an interview with Princess Diana that aired on the BBC in the United Kingdom, and "Dimbleby" is the author of a book on Prince Charles referenced in a key to the script. Numbers noted on the page refer to a bibliography of newspaper and magazine articles. The script page is provided by Victoria Bazely from the script by Cynthia Cherbak.

4. One writer (Tom Cook) explained it this way:

> You want to know what the archetypal TV movie is, particularly the NBC movie? We describe it as, "She was just like us, until . . ." You plug in what was unusual about her life. There's several things implicit in the first part of that. The first word, "she," means that most of the focus of these TV movies is about women and women's issues. And most of the network's divisions are run by women. The consensus is that that's the segment of the population that's watching them. They're programming to half the planet, basically. Ever wonder why men don't watch? The second part of it, "she was just like us," who's "us"? "Us" is upper-middle-class white women, living in the suburbs of the cities. It's not rural, full of black folks. So we have a distinct filter, here, on the American experience.

5. The network vice president (of movies and miniseries) in turn reports to the vice president of programming.

6. See appendix 1 for the statistics for the Kalamazoo, Michigan, area cable market for this period.

7. Elayne Rapping, for example, in a book-length study of made-for-television movies, considers the movie-of-the-week itself to be a "genre that tells a story about the family" (xl). There are, however, subclassifications, since later she states that there are "woman-in-danger TV films" (113).

8. See George Custen, *Bio/Pics* (New Brunswick, NJ: Rutgers UP, 1992): 18–22.

9. The titles in the sample include *The Positively True Adventures of the Alleged Texas Cheerleader-Murdering Mom* (1993); *Victim of Love: The Shannon Mohr Story* (1993); *Miracle Landing* (1990); *Voices Within: The Lives of Truddi Chase* (1990); *A Nightmare in Columbia County* (1991); *Beyond Control: The Amy Fisher Story* (1993); *Stay the Night* (1992), and *Desperate Rescue: The Cathy Mahone Story* (1993).

10. Writer/producer Cynthia Cherbak explains that she tries to find a "core concept" to focus her thinking in any project she writes because it is "something the audience can relate to," something that makes the purpose of the work accessible by making it "relatable to you and me."

11. Compare with the following observation from George Custen: "Viewers expect TV to present them with a dramatically engrossing explanation of a life recently in the news. The life need not be meritorious or instructive, as in the film biopic; it only has to be known" (*Bio/Pics* 220).

12. Jacques Lacan, *The Language of the Self,* trans. Anthony Wilden (New York: Dell, 1968). Here "identification" is the means of "internalization of the other" (160). Further, "Identification" is a fundamental component of Freudian theory, the

> operation itself whereby the human subject is constituted. This evolution is correlated chiefly, in the first place, with the coming to the fore of the Oedipus complex viewed in the light of its structural consequences, and secondly, with the revision effected by the second theory of the psychical apparatus, according to which those agencies that become differentiated from the id are given their specific characters by the identifications of which they are the outcome. (Laplanche and Pontalis 206)

13. Identification might best be thought of as "sympathy" rather than "empathy" with a character. Identification through sympathy allows us to feel commonality with a character without having to "become" that character entirely. For example, Carl Plantinga applies Murray Smith's notions of "alignment" and "allegiance" to explain the way *Unforgiven* allows a viewer to maintain an ambivalent relationship—to feel sympathetic toward and also distanced from—the violence of the film's main character, William Munny ("Spectacles" 70).

14. Identification is necessary for persuasion to occur; identification is a product of "consubstantiality," the ways we "ally ourselves with various properties of substances" so as to "share substance with whatever or whomever we associate" (Foss 158).

15. According to Bordwell, a "mode" is a means of presentation tied to "conventional or habitual usage" and "a historically distinct set of norms of narrational construction and comprehension" (150).

16. Besides Bordwell's *Classic Hollywood Cinema* and *Narration in the Fiction Film,* see Gomery. Gomery applies the defining characteristics of classic Hollywood narrative film form to the movie-of-the-week (207).

17. Throughout *Inside Prime Time,* Gitlin remarks on the political safety— the lack of risk taking—involved in telling victim stories. See his discussion of the cancellation of the *Lou Grant* series, for example (10). Subject matter is leveled out, made less risky, in order to avoid alienating any part of the target audience (181, 186).

18. The other victim here is Blanche, who, in order to exonerate her son, must force herself in full view of her family and friends to become a best friend to her son's seducer, the woman she hates most in the world.

19. Mike Kettman and Amy Fisher, for example, are given cars by their parents as demonstrations of love and trust, despite the problematic behavior of both children.

20. A character's movement through "jeopardy" in MOW "women in jeopardy" stories arguably entails "testing" as characters endure risk, transgress norms, and, as a result, undergo literal and figurative trials.

21. *Stay the Night* is the exception. This narrative uses straightforward chronology; however, it shifts its narrative viewpoint, halfway through, from son to mother. The question is not one of understanding what happened, as in the case of Shannon Mohr, but one of seeing what will happen as a result of Blanche's efforts.

22. The flashback clarifies the status of the present and looks forward as well. As Marcia Landy writes:

> The flashback serves to communicate information about the past—chronology, genealogy, motive, and the like—and this information can serve proleptically and teleologically to underscore determinism. Flashbacks, especially in biopics, often serve to create an organic sense of unfolding events and especially a sense of inevitability. (20–21)

23. The *Miracle Landing* passengers are the exception to this rule of transgression and trial. They simply have had the bad luck to be on a plane that begins to disintegrate in mid-flight. The trial they undergo tests their courage and abilities to cope with this extraordinary adversity.

24. "Headline concept" can be "high concept" and at the same time affords safety of subject in covering real events. See Gitlin 79.

25. George Custen suggests that trials

> lay bare the specific messages of the biopic, encasing one narrative within another on a parallel level of commentary. The presence of trials suggests the purpose of the biopic is to offer up a lesson or judgment in the form of a movie. (*Bio/Pics* 186)

26. A detailed synopsis of the film appears in appendix 3.

27. We learn that Davis has told Jeri, his girlfriend before and after Shannon's death, that he is a secret government agent, and that he has other women in his life call him "Cappy." The name becomes a way of eventually identifying and capturing him.

28. Restoring the moral order here involves an implicit return to the balance that was disrupted at the beginning of the narration, when Dave Davis entered their lives. The film ends with Bob and Lucille Mohr visiting Shannon's grave. The name on the stone has been changed from "Shannon Davis" to "Shannon Mohr." Bob Mohr takes his wife's arm and suggests that now they can "go home."

29. "Wanda Holloway puts all her energy into promotion, instead of putting it into skill. With you, I emphasize skill, that's why you're so successful," Verna tells her daughter, while Wanda is advising Shanna, "People like that, you've got to pity them."

30. The idea that the medium of television is inherently "postmodern" is not new. Jane Feuer, for example, has suggested that "what is postmodern in television is textuality generally" (9). Part of what Feuer sees as important about the textual referentiality of late-1980s/early-1990s MOW docudrama will also be relevant here: The foregrounding of text(s) becomes integral to arguments for empowerment that the works advocate. Similarly, John Caldwell points to texts as the "vernacular" of television (5).

31. Bill Nichols argues that the sense of communal information imparted by reality TV programming is illusory. Recreation produces de-authentication:

> Reality TV offers communion drawn from atomized, dissociated figures who remain so; a sense of engagement, empathy, charity, and hope built on a disengaged, detached simulation of face-to-face encounter; and a sense of coherence and continuity, if not suspended animation, at a time when ideas and values feel worn, ineffective, abused, and bandied about. (*Boundaries* 56–57)

32. These include recreated interview sessions with Bob and Lucille Mohr, Dick Britton and his wife (the Davis's neighbors), and Tracy Lien, Shannon Mohr's cousin.

6. Recent Feature Film Docudrama as Persuasive Practice

1. See comments by Charles Freericks, NBC executive, cited in chapter 5.

2. *Patch Adams* grossed $134,800,000 through April 1999 (*Variety* 4 May 1999: 13).

3. Stanley Kauffman similarly observes that "for once, the focus of a Mafia film is mostly on a laborer in the ranks—a killer, with twenty-six hits to his credit, but after all these years still just a low-income laborer" (26).

4. For background on the suppression of the story, see *Jet* 25 Apr. 1994: 12; R. Thomas Dye, "The Rosewood Massacre: History and the Making of Public Policy," *Public Historian* 19 (Summer 1997): 25–39; and John Taylor, "The Rosewood Massacre," *Esquire* 122 July 1994: 46–54.

5. Given the limited business *Rosewood* did at the box office, it is difficult to determine the extent to which this perspective might be valid. According to *Variety's* weekly box office reports throughout 1997, *Rosewood* and *Ghosts of Mississippi* grossed the lowest of the films in the group ($13 million each) compared to, for example, *Amistad* ($44.2 million), and *Donnie Brasco* ($42 million).

6. These included Edward Ball, *Slaves in the Family;* Hugh Thomas, *The Slave Trade,* and Velma Thomas, *Lest We Forget.*

7. *Ryan* had earned over $214 million as of April 1999 (*Variety* 20 Apr. 1999: 10).

8. The editorial stated, in part:

The clear burden of her suit and commentary is that the unattributed borrowing of plot elements is theft, while the unattributed, unmarked quotation of passages from a nonfiction book is merely a matter of words. That is a distinction without a difference. The very protection Ms. Chase-Riboud insists upon is undermined by her own practice. No artistic license can justify that. (Klinkenborg A18)

Works Cited

Agee, James. *Agee on Film*. New York: McDowell, Obelensky, 1958.

Alter, Jonathan. "The Long Shadow of Slavery." *Newsweek* 8 Dec. 1997: 58–63.

Amistad. Dir. Steven Spielberg. Dreamworks SKG, 1997.

Ansen, David. "*Amistad*." *Newsweek* 8 Dec. 1997: 64–65.

Arthur, Paul. "Jargons of Authenticity (Three American Moments)." Renov 108–34.

At First Sight. Dir. Irwin Winkler. MGM, 1999.

Beyond Control: The Amy Fisher Story. Dir. Andy Tennant. ABC Productions, 1993.

Bordwell, David. *Narration in the Fiction Film*. Madison: U of Wisconsin P, 1985.

Bordwell, David, Janet Staiger, and Kristin Thompson. *The Classical Hollywood Cinema: Film Style and Mode of Production to 1960*. New York: Columbia UP, 1985.

Brooks, Peter. *The Melodramatic Imagination*. New Haven: Yale UP, 1974.

Burke, Kenneth, *A Rhetoric of Motives*. Berkeley: U of California P, 1969.

Cable, Mary. *Black Odyssey: The Case of the Slave Ship Amistad*. New York: Viking, 1971.

Caldwell, Dave. Personal interview. March 1997.

Caldwell, John T. *Televisuality: Style, Crisis, and Authority in American Television*. New Brunswick, NJ: Rutgers UP, 1995.

Call Northside 777. Dir. Henry Hathaway. Twentieth Century–Fox, 1948.

Carr, Jay. "Uplifting Tale of Time and Space." *Boston Globe* 19 Feb. 1999: D4.

Carter, Bill, "Rebound for Broadcast TV." *New York Times* 20 Apr. 1994: D1.

Cherbak, Cynthia. Personal interview. March 1997.

A Civil Action. Dir. Steven Zaillian. Paramount, 1998.

Cook, Tom. Personal interview. March 1997.

Corner, John. *The Art of Records: A Critical Introduction to Documentary*. New York: Manchester UP, 1996.

Custen, George F. *Bio/Pics*. New Brunswick, NJ: Rutgers UP, 1992.

———. *Twentieth Century's Fox: Darryl F. Zanuck and the Culture of Hollywood*. New York: Basic, 1998.

Davis, Thulani. "Civil Rights and Wrongs." *American Film* 14 Dec. 1988: 32–38+.

Denby, David. "Popular Mechanic." *New Yorker* 22 Feb.–1 Mar. 1999: 184–86.

————. "Porn Again." *New York* 23–30 Dec. 1996: 146+.

Desperate Rescue: The Cathy Mahone Story. Dir. Richard A. Colla. World International Network, 1993.

Donnie Brasco. Dir. Mike Newell. TriStar, 1997.

Dye, R. Thomas. "The Rosewood Massacre: History and the Making of Public Policy. " *Public Historian* 19 (Summer 1997): 25–39.

Edgar, David, "Theatre of Fact: A Dramatist's Viewpoint," *Why Docudrama?* Ed. Alan Rosenthal. Carbondale: Southern Illinois UP, 1999.

Edgerton, Gary, "High Concept Small Screen." *Journal of Popular Film and Television* 19.3 (1991): 114–27.

Farley, Christopher John. "Soul Food." *Time* 13 Oct. 1997: 86–88.

Feuer, Jane. *Seeing Through the Eighties: Television and Reaganism.* Durham: Duke UP, 1995.

Foner, Eric. "Amistad." *New York Times* 20 Dec. 1997: A13.

Foss, Sonja K., Karen A. Foss, and Robert Trapp. *Contemporary Perspectives on Rhetoric.* Prospect Heights, IL: Waveland, 1985.

Freedman, Samuel. "Laying Claim to Sorrow Beyond Words." *New York Times* 13 Dec. 1997: B7+.

Freericks, Charles. Vice President of Movies and Miniseries, NBC. Letter to the author. 29 Apr. 1997.

French, Sean. "Parker's Brand." *Sight and Sound* 58.2 (1989): 132–33.

Ghosts of Mississippi. Dir. Rob Reiner. Columbia Pictures, 1996.

Gitlin, Todd. *Inside Prime Time.* New York: Pantheon, 1983.

Gomery, Douglas. "*Brian's Song:* Television, Hollywood, and the Evolution of the Movie Made For Television." *Television: The Critical View.* Ed. Horace Newcomb. 4th ed. New York: Oxford UP, 1987. 197–220.

Goodwin, Richard N. *Remembering America: A Voice from the Sixties.* Boston: Little, 1988.

Grindon, Leger. *Shadows of the Past—Studies in the Historical Fiction Film.* Philadelphia: Temple UP, 1994.

Hilary and Jackie. Dir. Anand Tucker. October Films, 1998.

Hirsh, Foster. *The Darkside of the Screen: Film Noir.* New York: Barnes, 1981.

Hoffer, Tom W., and Richard Alan Nelson. "Docudrama on American Television." Rosenthal, *Why Docudrama?* 64–77.

Holland, Norman N. *The Dynamics of Literary Response.* New York: Norton, 1975.

The House on 92nd Street. Dir. Henry Hathaway. Twentieth Century–Fox, 1945.

The Hurricane. Dir. Norman Jewison. Universal, 1999.

In the Name of the Father. Dir. Jim Sheridan. Universal Pictures, 1993.

Jackson, Donald Dale. "Mutiny on the *Amistad.*" *Smithsonian* 28 (Dec. 1997): 114–18.

James, Caryn. "Cable TV Cashes in on Current Film Crop." *New York Times* 16 Dec. 1997: E1+.

JFK. Dir. Oliver Stone. Warner Bros., 1991.

Karp, Walter. "The Quiz-Show Scandal." *American Heritage* (May–June 1989): 88.

Kauffmann, Stanley. "Scanning Cultures." *The New Republic* 31 Mar. 1997: 26–27.

Klawans, Stuart. "Craft Warnings." *The Nation* 31 Mar. 1997: 35–36.

Klinkenborg, Verlyn. "The Limits of Artistic License." *New York Times* 23 Dec. 1997: A18.

Landy, Marcia. *Cinematic Uses of the Past.* Minneapolis: U of Minnesota P, 1996.

Lang, Robert. *American Film Melodrama: Griffith, Vidor, Minelli.* Princeton: Princeton UP, 1989.

Laplanche, J., and J.-B. Pontalis. *The Language of Psycho-analysis.* Trans. Donald Nicholson-Smith. New York: Norton, 1973. 206.

Leab, Daniel. "The Moving Image as Interpreter of History: Telling the Dancer from the Dance." *Image as Artifact: The Historical Analysis of Film and Television.* Ed. John O'Connor. Malabar, FL: Krieger, 1990. 69–95.

A League of Their Own. Dir. Penny Marshall. Columbia Pictures, 1992.

Leo, John. "JQA: Hollywood Hunk." *U.S. News and World Report* 12 Jan. 1999: 12.

Loke, Margarett. "Writer Who Cried Plagiarism Used Passages She Didn't Write." *New York Times* 19 Dec. 1997: A1+.

Maher, Kevin. "October Sky." *Sight and Sound* 10.1 (2000): 59–60.

Maslin, Janet. "A Black Man Accused, A Town Destroyed." *New York Times* 21 Feb. 1997: C18.

———. "Eyes Toward the Stars." *New York Times* 19 Feb. 1999: E14.

———. "Oliver Stone Manipulates His Puppet." *New York Times* 5 Jan. 1992.

Mead, Rebecca. "One Novelist, Two Screenwriters, and Confusion Aboard the Amistad." *New Yorker* 1 Dec. 1997: 37–38.

Mifflin, Lawrie. "Cable TV Continues Its Steady Drain of Network Viewers." *New York Times* 25 Oct. 1995: C13.

Miles, Margaret Ruth. "Larry Flynt in Real Life." *Christian Century* 23–30 Apr. 1997: 419–20.

Millar, Jeff. "Rocket Science." *Houston Chronicle* 19 Feb. 1999: 1.

Miller, Bruce. Personal interview. March 1997.

Miracle Landing. Dir. Dick Lowry. CBS Entertainment, 1990.

Mississippi Burning. Dir. Alan Parker. Orion, 1988.

Music of the Heart. Dir. Wes Craven. Miramax, 1999.

Nemec, Dennis. Personal interview. March 1997.

Nichols, Bill. *Blurred Boundaries.* Bloomington: Indiana UP, 1994.

———. *Representing Reality.* Bloomington: Indiana UP, 1991.

A Nightmare in Columbia County. Dir. Roger Young. Landsburg Co., 1991.

October Sky. Dir. Joe Johnston. Universal, 1999.

Owens, William A. *Black Mutiny.* Philadelphia: Pilgrims, 1968.

Paget, Derek. *No Other Way to Tell It: Dramadoc/Docudrama in Television.* Manchester: Manchester UP, 1998.

Patch Adams. Dir. Tom Shadyac. Universal, 1998.

Peirce, C. S. *Philosophical Writings of Peirce.* Ed. J. Buchler. New York: Dover, 1955.

The People Vs. Larry Flynt. Dir. Milos Forman. Columbia Pictures, 1996.

Plantinga, Carl R. *Rhetoric and Representation in Nonfiction Film.* New York: Cambridge UP, 1997.

———. "Spectacles of Death: Clint Eastwood and Violence in *Unforgiven.*" *Cinema Journal* 37.2 (1998): 70.

Podhoretz, Norman. "'Lolita,' My Mother-in-Law, the Marquis de Sade, and Larry Flynt." *Commentary* 103 (Apr. 1997): 23–35.

The Positively True Adventures of the Alleged Texas Cheerleader-Murdering Mom. Dir. Michael Ritchie. HBO, 1993.

Powdermaker, Hortense. *Hollywood: The Dream Factory: An Anthropologist Looks at the Movie-Makers.* Boston: Little, 1950.

Quiz Show. Dir. Robert Redford. Buena Vista Pictures, 1994.

Rael, Patrick. "The Freedom Struggle Film: Hollywood or History?" *Socialist Review* 22 (July 1992): 119–30.

Rafferty, Terrance. "Playing with Fire." *New Yorker* 2 Dec. 1996: 116–19.

Rainer, Tristine. Personal interview. March 1997.

Rapping, Elayne. *The Movie of the Week.* Minneapolis: U of Minnesota P, 1990.

Rayner, Richard. "Movies." *Harper's Bazaar* Dec. 1996: 116.

Renov, Michael, ed. *Theorizing Documentary.* New York: Routledge, 1993.

Rice, Lynette. "NBC Wins; Fox Grows." *Broadcasting and Cable* (3 Mar. 1997): 5.

Rich, Frank. "Who Stole History?" *New York Times* 13 Dec. 1997: A15.

Rosen, Philip. "Document and Documentary: On the Persistence of Historical Concepts." Renov 58–89.

Rosenstone, Robert. *Revisioning History.* Princeton: Princeton UP, 1995.

———. *Visions of the Past.* Cambridge: Harvard UP, 1995.

Rosenthal, Alan, ed. *Why Docudrama?* Carbondale: Southern Illinois UP, 1999.

———. *Writing Docudrama.* Boston: Focal, 1995.

Rosewood. Dir. John Singleton. Warner Bros., 1997.

Rybocki, Karen, and D. J. Rybocki. *Advocacy and Opposition.* Englewood Cliffs: Prentice-Hall, 1991.

Sarris, Andrew. *The American Cinema.* New York: Dutton, 1968.

Schickel, Richard. "Rosewood." *Time* 3 Mar. 1997: 83.

Schindler's List. Dir. Steven Spielberg. Amblin Entertainment, 1993.

Shannon Mohr: A Victim of Love. Dir. John Cosgrove. Cosgrove/Meurer, 1993.

Shargel, Raphael. "Amistad." *The New Leader* 26 Jan. 1998: 18–19.

Shine. Dir. Scott Hicks. Fine Line, 1996.

Shipp, E. R. "Taking Control of Old Demons by Forcing Them into the Light." *New York Times* 16 Mar. 1997: 13+.

Smith, Gavin. "Mississippi Gambler." *Film Comment* 24.4 (1988): 26–30.

Sohmer, Steve. Personal interview. March 1997.

Solomon, Aubry. *Twentieth Century Fox: A Corporate and Financial History.* Metuchen, NJ: Scarecrow, 1988.

Sorlin, Pierre. *The Film in History: Restaging the Past.* Totowa, NJ: Barnes, 1980.

Stay the Night. Dir. Harry Winer. New World Productions, 1992.

Steinem, Gloria. "Hollywood Cleans Up *Hustler.*" *New York Times* 7 Jan. 1997: A17.

Sterling, Victoria. Personal interview. March 1997.

Strickler, Jeff. "Tribute to the American Can-Do Spirit." *Star Tribune* 19 Feb. 1999: O1E.

Telotte, J. P. "Outside the System: The Documentary Voice of Film Noir." *New Orleans Review* 14.2 (1987): 55–63.

13 Rue Madeleine. Dir. Henry Hathaway. Twentieth Century–Fox, 1946.

Tuska, Jon. *Dark Cinema: American Film Noir in Cultural Perspective.* Westport, CT: Greenwood, 1984.

Voices Within: The Lives of Truddi Chase. Dir. Lamont Johnson. New World Television, 1990.

Weinraub, Bernard. "Filmmakers of *Amistad* Rebut Claim by Novelist." *New York Times* 4 Dec. 1997: E1+.

White, Armond. "Against the Hollywood Grain." *Film Comment* 34 (Mar./Apr. 1998): 34–42.

White, Hayden. *The Content of the Form.* Baltimore: Johns Hopkins UP, 1989.

Wollen, Peter. *Signs and Meaning in the Cinema.* Bloomington: Indiana UP, 1972.

Index

Steven N. Lipkin teaches film at Western Michigan University, where he is an associate professor in the Department of Communication. He has published essays on the phenomenology of video and on film melodrama. His research on feature film and movie-of-the-week docudrama continues.